A Treasury
of Rūmī

THE TREASURY SERIES IN
ISLAMIC THOUGHT AND CIVILISATION

Muhammad Isa Waley

❧ ❧ ❧

كـنوز من الرومي

A Treasury
of Rūmī

Guidance on the Path of
Wisdom and Unity

KUBE
PUBLISHING

*A Treasury of Rūmī: Guidance on the Path
of Wisdom and Unity*

First published in England by
Kube Publishing Ltd,
Markfield Conference Centre,
Ratby Lane, Markfield,
Leicestershire LE67 9SY,
United Kingdom.

TEL: +44 (0)1530 249230
FAX: +44 (0)1530 249656
WEBSITE: www.kubepublishing.com
EMAIL: info@kubepublishing.com

CIP data for this book is available from the British Library.

ISBN 978-1-84774-102-8 casebound
ISBN 978-1-84774-105-9 ebook

Cover design: Inspiral Design
Book design: Imtiaze Ahmed
Persian, Arabic & English typeset: nqaddoura@hotmail.com

Printed in Turkey by Elma Basim

Contents

WINGS TO FLY WITH: FEAR, HOPE, AND LOVE

BITTER AND SWEET: SELF-DISCIPLINE AND SPIRITUAL PROGRESS

FAITH AND WISDOM: THE DĪN OF ISLAM FROM WITHIN

ASPECTS OF UNITY: WISDOM, KNOWLEDGE, SERENITY

Transliteration Table

Arabic Consonants

Initial, unexpressed medial and final: ء ʾ

ا	a	د	d	ض	ḍ	ك	k
ب	b	ذ	dh	ط	ṭ	ل	l
ت	t	ر	r	ظ	ẓ	م	m
ث	th	ز	z	ع	ʿ	ن	n
ج	j	س	s	غ	gh	هـ	h
ح	ḥ	ش	sh	ف	f	و	w
خ	kh	ص	ṣ	ق	q	ي	y

With a *shaddah*, both medial and final consonants are doubled.

Vowels, diphthongs, etc.

Short: ـَ a   ـِ i   ـُ u

Long: ـَا ā   ـِي ī   ـُو ū

Diphthongs: ـَوْ aw
                        ـَىْ ay

Introduction

❧ ❧ ❧

A few decades ago, few people would have required evidence that Mawlānā Jalāl al-Dīn Muḥammad ibn Muḥammad, known to many today simply as 'Rūmī', was a serious Muslim. But nowadays, many of the published presentations of his work and thought seem concerned in showing this great Islamic scholar, teacher and saint as 'the acceptable face of Islam': a mediaeval Muslim civilized and humanistic enough to know how to keep Islam in its proper place, so to speak. (To say this is not to deny that Mawlānā Rūmī is a highly appropriate voice for Islam in this day and age.) Moreover, some of the English interpretations of his work that have sold in large numbers are skilfully written but seriously inaccurate. In extreme cases, they evoke an image of a Rūmī who embraced, far ahead of his time, some of the heresies and vices most detested in normative Islam. The version of Jalāl al-Dīn that became 'the best-selling poet in North America today' is not altogether authentic. As he himself writes, in one of the first lines of his masterpiece, the *Mathnawī-i maʿnawī*: 'Everyone has, in their view, become my close friend / but they have not sought out the secrets within me.' By contrast with this contrived image of a 'New Age Rūmī', this book aims to prove and illustrate, by presenting relevant texts in translation, the thoroughly traditional basis of the teachings of a man whose personal name (*ism*) is that of the Prophet, may Allah bless him and grant him peace; and whose honorary title (*laqab*) means 'Majesty of the Faith'.

That is not, however, the sole purpose of this book. For many Muslims and non-Muslims, the current discourse concerning Islam is so dominated by concerns to do with extremism and terrorism that little time or space is left to consider the central aspects of the *Dīn*, these being the relationships between each individual human being and (i) his or her Lord and Cherisher, the Master and Owner of the entire universe; (ii) the Emissary of God, to whom he or she addresses greetings in every prayer; (iii) the rest of humankind, to whom the *Dīn* assigns us a hierarchy of obligations; and (iv) our mother and temporary home, the Earth, and all its creatures. The faith of Islam as conveyed by the Seal of the Prophets, may God exalt and preserve him, has an abundance of teachings on all these subjects. Since his time it has been and remains the duty of his inheritors, the people of sacred learning, to safeguard, propagate and explain those teachings. Prominent among these people have been the masters of the science of *Taṣawwuf* (Sufism), the subject matter of which is the purification of the self and *iḥsān*, or excellence, in worshipping and serving God Most High wholeheartedly and with sincere intentions, and in coming to know and have a close relationship with the Lord and Cherisher of all Existence. To strive to achieve such excellence to the very best of one's ability is to fulfil the purpose for which humankind was created.

The aim in compiling this *Treasury* has been to present a small but telling selection of excerpts from the teachings of Mawlānā Rūmī, representing the variety of broad themes and types of discourse to be found in them. The easiest way to achieve this would have been to confine oneself to the prose works, which are in general the most accessible to the modern reader. Moreover, the format of the *Treasury* series calls for excerpts that are brief, and the more discursive nature of Rūmī's verse narratives and teaching makes it difficult to find passages that are not only concise but also 'self-contained'. It also precludes the inclusion of the longer narratives characteristic of the *Mathnawī*.

To omit the poetical works entirely, however, would have been a disservice not to only to the author but also to the reader. Many Muslims today are brought up and educated having little contact with poetry, and consequently may find it more challenging to follow, understand and fully appreciate the points being made. *Inshallah* the comments attached to each excerpt will help them to understand, contextualize, and benefit from the content. In addition, while a rhyming and rhythmic text is easier to memorize, part of the wisdom behind imparting teachings in verse form is to demand more of the reader. Making the effort to interpret, engage with, and absorb them may aid retention or memorization. The same can be said of the Holy Qur'an, which demands our attention and effort, as well as evokes wonder in us, by employing parables, symbols and metaphors with miraculous power and eloquence. The words of Rūmī cannot be placed on the same level as the Qur'an, but many passages in his *Mathnawī* and other works are in effect pieces of Qur'anic commentary, as we shall see.

The following abbreviations have been used in referring to sources:

D	*Dīwān-i kabīr (Kulliyyāt-i Shams);*
DOR	*Discourses of Rūmī;*
FMF	*Fīh mā fīh;*
M	*Mathnawī;*
MS	*Majālis-i sabʿa;*
SOTU	*Signs of the Unseen.*

The Life and Times of Jalāl al-Dīn Rūmī

Historical Background

The seventh century AH (thirteenth century CE) was a time of immense turmoil in Central and Western Asia. The cataclysm of the Mongol invasion and conquest, a turning point in history, had as great an impact on these particular regions as on any other. The Seljuks of Rūm, the ruling dynasty in much of Asia Minor, often suffered from weak governance and internecine conflict. It was part of the Sufis' mission to try to improve the lot of ordinary people by influencing the rulers in the direction of compassion and fair taxation and rule. Here both Mawlānā Jalāl al-Dīn and his son and successor Sulṭān Walad played an important role.

Part 1: The Religious Scholar

Jalāl al-Dīn Muḥammad ibn Muḥammad was born in 604/1207, either in the town of Vakhsh (in today's Tajikistan) or possibly in Balkh, Afghanistan. His background was learned, Persian-speaking, and Sunni. His father, Bahā' al-Dīn Walad, was a religious scholar and mystic whose Meditations (*Maʿārif*), distinctive (and sometimes daring) personal meditations rich in imagery, clearly influenced his son. In about 619/1219, probably because of the threat of invasion by the Mongols, the family travelled west to Baghdad, then performed Hajj. Like many who had emigrated from the East, they then proceeded to Asia Minor, living in various towns for some years before finally settling in Konya. By this time Jalāl al-Dīn and his wife Gawhar Khātūn, whom he had married at the age of eighteen, had two sons. In 628/1231, Bahā' al-Dīn died and was succeeded in his teaching post by Jalāl al-Dīn, now an expert in the Islamic sciences.

The following year, Burhān al-Dīn Muḥaqqiq Tirmidhī, a former disciple of Bahā' al-Dīn Walad, arrived in Konya to supervise Jalāl's further training. Under the guidance of Burhān, whose Persian discourses (*Maʿārif*) are too little known, the young scholar travelled the spiritual path of Sufism, graduated from the hard school of asceticism (*zuhd*) and spiritual retreat (*khalwa*), and enhanced his learning and experience through two periods of study in Syria. While there he encountered some of the leading Sufis of the day and became familiar with Arabic poetry. This period ended with Burhān al-Dīn's death in 638/1240. Jalāl al-Dīn was by now a respected scholar and preacher in Konya, in Sufism as well as in Ḥanafī jurisprudence and other religious sciences. In time he gained influence among the most important political figures of the day. Some came to visit and learn from him, and with others he corresponded.

The Sun of Truth

The event that revolutionized Rūmī's life has since indirectly influenced the lives of multitudes. In 642/1244 a wandering dervish named Shams al-Dīn Tabrīzī arrived in Konya. In their first encounter, Shams showed Jalāl al-Dīn that there were whole realms of knowledge and experience that had been closed to him. Each found that in the other's company and guidance a door to new spiritual realization had opened. Intoxicated with this love, Jalāl al-Dīn no longer cared what others thought. The radiance of Shams's presence was, it seemed to him, barely separable from the radiance of God Himself. Had not the Prophet Jacob suffered inexpressible sorrow and became almost blind from weeping at the loss of his son Joseph, that peerless reflection of Divine Beauty? For over a year, Jalāl al-Dīn and Shams were almost constantly together. Because of things that certain people have written, it needs to be spelled out that this was a Divinely willed, platonic friendship: two complementary spiritual types of exceptional stature, each learning from and devoted to the other. It is clear from the sources that Shams was the more *jalālī* (rigorous and majestic) of the two and Jalāl al-Dīn the more *jamālī* (mild and serene).

Many of those who venerated Jalāl al-Dīn were at a loss to understand the transformation of their master into a man intoxicated with love of the Divine, who composed poetry while turning round and round. Then one day Shams suddenly vanished, fleeing the jealousy of his companion's disciples. Jalāl al-Dīn was distraught, as we learn from the sources (including poems) in which he pleads with his friend to return. His loyal son Sulṭān Walad was sent to find him, and eventually brought him back from Damascus to Konya. Not long afterwards, however, Shams disappeared again – this time for good.

Who was this Shams al-Dīn Tabrīzī? Besides the testimony of Rūmī's biographers, his collected sayings (*Maqālāt*) have also survived. Shams was an educated man, a Shāfiʿī who had studied jurisprudence in depth. It was part of his way as a Sufi to conceal his true nature from others, shunning respectability and diplomatic behaviour. We learn from the *Maqālāt* that the main purpose of Shams's travels was to find a true Friend of God (*Walī Allāh*), or saint. In *Maqāla* 685 he describes his first meeting with Jalāl al-Dīn Rūmī, when Shams questioned him about the Persian Sufi Bāyazīd Basṭāmī and why he had not found it necessary to say to God, as the Blessed Prophet himself had said, 'We have not known You as You deserve to be known.' The *Maqālāt* also reveal how greatly Shams admired Jalāl al-Dīn as a scholar and spiritual figure who possessed qualities that he did not – but that Shams was also a teacher to him and so the relationship was not of the normal type between master and disciple.

Although the loss of his teacher grieved him, as a spiritual master Mawlānā knew well that everything that is worth loving is to be found to perfection in the Divine Beloved. But Shams al-Dīn had demanded of him everything he had, in order that he transcend the bounds of conventional piety in the quest for complete experiential vision and illumination. What he mourned so eloquently was the loss of that overwhelming inner sunlight, and the companion – a scruffy, boorish impostor in the eyes of many, but for him the Perfect Guide – who had completed his spiritual direction and continually inspired him.

Later Life

As time passed the impact of the trauma waned. Whatever Shams had essentially represented to him Jalāl al-Dīn now found within himself and in close companions like Ṣalāḥ al-Dīn Zarkūb, a simple, pure-hearted goldsmith from the bazaar of Konya; and Ḥusām al-Dīn Chalabī, a saintly individual who was a faithful and capable helper to his teacher and the chief inspiration of the latter's masterpiece, the *Mathnawī*. His equilibrium thus regained, Rūmī lived on for over twenty years, supervising the training of disciples and teaching through discourses, letters, and poetry. His death in 672/1273 was mourned not only by Muslims but also by Konya's large Christian population. The direction of the brotherhood passed into the hands of Ḥusām al-Dīn, and then to Jalāl al-Dīn's son Sulṭān Walad. Founder of what would become the Mawlawī, or Mevlevi, Sufi Order (*Ṭarīqa*), Walad was also an able administrator and an author; his works include discourses, a *Dīwān*, and some long poems including a valuable account of his father's life.

WORKS

Discourses (*Fīhi mā fīh*)

The best known prose work associated with Rūmī is the collection of discourses known by the Arabic title *Fīhi mā fīh* (meaning 'What's in it is in it', or possibly 'Whatever there is, is in it'). The text as we have it today was compiled from records (or recollections) of the Master's teachings with disciples and admirers who attended his gatherings. Most of the main themes explored in the *Mathnawī* are also touched on in the Discourses. Sometimes, as in the *Mathnawī*, he moves back and forth between one point and another related one, interweaving narrative and commentary. For readers who are less familiar or comfortable with poetry, perhaps because of the overwhelmingly prosaic education prevalent in these days of techno-domination, the Discourses may offer a more accessible introduction to the teachings of the Master of Konya.

Sermons (*Majālis-i Sabʿa*)

The other prose work attributable to Mawlānā is called *Majālis-i Sabʿa* (literally, 'Seven Sessions'). It comprises seven homilies of varying length, which may have been addressed to a general audience, not to Sufis only. Judging by their style and content, most or all were delivered before the encounter with Shams. Each *Majlis* begins with praise of God in Arabic, normally in rhyming prose (*sajʿ*), and continues with *duʿāʾ* or supplicatory prayers, at least partly in Persian. Some begin with a Hadith or Tradition of the Prophet (*ṣallā Allāh ʿalayh wa sallam*), which is then paraphrased in Persian and commented upon at length before the speaker moves on to related topics, often with stories to illustrate the points being made. The *Majālis* contain a much higher proportion of verses – up to twenty couplets at a time – than the *Fīh mā fīh* discourses. This suggests that the speaker was already a connoisseur of mystical poetry, although some of the verses may have been inserted later by the compiler of the text. Besides those found in Mawlānā's own *Dīwān* there are also quotations from his predecessors Sanā'ī and ʿAṭṭār, amongst others.

Letters (*Maktūbāt*)

Of Jalāl al-Dīn Rūmī's 145 surviving letters, most were written or dictated to influential people, mainly to request favours on behalf of friends or relatives. Several are addressed to the Parwāna Muʿīn al-Dīn, a powerful local official, or to his Georgian wife

Gurjī Khātūn. A good number are addressed to the writer's son Sulṭān Walad, and these are extremely affectionate. Some of the letters contain short passages of spiritual guidance. An interesting feature of the *Maktūbāt* is the presence of invocations and interjections in Arabic or in Persian. While some of these are of the kind one might find in any pious Islamic literature, others are more unconventional: for example, the name Allah simply repeated several times (probably a form of admonition meaning, roughly, 'Be sure to give God His due'). Besides these prose letters, a few in verse form have also survived; one example is included in this book.

Poetical works: *Dīwān-i kabīr*

Rūmī's lyric poetry has the intensity of a man who has given everything, lost everything – and found everything. The poems collected in the *Dīwān*, which as the earliest manuscripts indicate were originally entitled *Dīwān-i Shams al-Ḥaqā'iq* or *Dīwān-i Kabīr* (the Great *Dīwān*), comprise about 40,000 verses. Composed probably over a period of more than thirty years, they were sometimes chanted at the gatherings of Mevlevi dervishes. Besides ghazals, there are also quatrains and longer stanzaic poems. Most are in praise of love of the Divine and the ecstasy of lovers 'crazy' enough to give everything in their quest for the Beloved. They evoke, often with tremendous poetic force, a variety of spiritual states; closeness to God, longing, separation, hope, fear, self-reproach, exultation. Some also contain narratives with morals, though in briefer form than in the *Mathnawī*. This *Treasury* contains less of Mawlānā's ecstatic poetry than other selections do; purely in order to strike a balance, not because of any partiality on the compiler's part.

Mawlānā claimed that he did not care for poetry and that he only composed it to please his local audience, who did not have the same liking for sermons as people in his native region, Central Asia. Arberry, following the rhetoric of Sulṭān Walad's account of his father, has been followed by others in asserting that Jalāl al-Dīn was 'wholly incapable of controlling the torrent of poetry that poured forth from him.' But many poems in the *Dīwān* display control and technical mastery as well as eloquence and ingenuity. For example, one of the long stanzaic poems or *Tarjīʿāt* comprises seven stanzas of twelve couplets, and their coherence and technical precision are exemplary. Prosodically, Rūmī used a wider variety of meters than any other Persian poet. Linguistically, he also wrote some poems wholly in Arabic, some partly in Arabic and partly in Persian, some lines in Turkish, and a few in Demotic Greek. All this shows that he had studied assiduously the works of other masters of Persian and Arabic verse. In poetry, as in all crafts, mastery is rarely achieved (even by geniuses), without prolonged study and sheer hard work. Finally, the range of his imagery and symbolism testifies to an extraordinary power of unitive vision.

Poetical works: The *Mathnawī*

The *Mathnawī* is the author's undisputed masterpiece. This extraordinary poem, which is a kind of literary treatise in rhyming couplets on Islamic spirituality, is immensely long, comprising over 25,000 verses in six *Daftar*s, or volumes. It appears that its composition was inspired by a suggestion from his 'star disciple' Ḥusām al-Dīn Chalabī that the master produce a work like the *Ilāhī-nāma* or 'Book of God', a didactic poem by the great Persian Sufi ʿAṭṭār that was popular among some of Mawlānā's disciples. And that is what he did, expressing the hope that after his passing the *Mathnawī* itself would be like a Shaykh to take his place (though he taught that guidance from a living spiritual master was also indispensable). Seven centuries and a half later, that hope has been amply fulfilled. What a providential aspiration, and what manifest success! Precisely when the composition of the *Mathnawī* began is not known, but it must have been in or near to 660/1260. The process continued until the author's death thirteen years later, with a break after completion of the first *Daftar*.

Those who know Arabic may be interested to read the prefaces (in that language) to five of the six Books. Each deals with one or two key themes. The fifth, for example, comments on the relationship between the Sacred Law (*Sharīʿa*), Inner Reality (*Ḥaqīqa*), and the Way (*Ṭarīqa*). The great Sufi poet and metaphysician ʿAbd al-Raḥmān Jāmī (d. 895/1492) nicknamed the *Mathnawī* 'the Qur'an in Persian'. This is of course poetic hyperbole; but the poem certainly offers, amongst other things, profound commentaries on many passages of the Holy Qur'an. In that connection the author himself makes a crucial point: when reading or hearing about Moses and Pharaoh, one should beware of thinking that this is no more than 'a tale of the ancients'. At a deeper level it is an account of the conflict between Truth and falsehood that takes place within human souls; other Qur'anic narratives, too, have universal significations.

The notion advanced by orientalists that the *Mathnawī* is rambling and lacks coherence is a serious error, for while the connecting thread may at times be subtle, time and again two or more themes are skilfully interwoven, left suspended for a page or two, and then resumed. The same criticism has been levelled at the ghazals of the great Persian lyric poet Ḥāfiẓ. Such views illustrate the difficulty many westerners have in fully appreciating literary works from other cultures.

The *Mathnawī*'s stories come from many sources. There was a rich seam of folk tales to be mined in the written and oral traditions of Central Asia and the Middle East. Certain stories, for example, are derived from *Kalīla wa Dimna*, animal fables that are largely of Indian origin. Others, such as the now famous story of the elephant in a dark room, can be found in the poems of Rūmī's predecessor Sanā'ī. Many of the narratives, however, are derived from the Holy Qur'an and stories of the Prophets, the *Awliyā' Allāh* ('Friends of God' or saints), their struggles and triumphs, and their relationships with their Lord and their fellow creatures. Although most of the tales in the *Mathnawī* are not original, the poet's treatment of them often is. Between them come passages in which the moral is dwelt upon – another possible reason for the analogies made with Islam's Holy Book.

This *Treasury of Rūmī* cannot claim any degree of comprehensiveness. To enable readers to pick and choose between general themes, however, the content has been divided into ten sections, each comprising seven texts: (1) Who are We? The Nature and Origin of Mankind; (2) Facing Facts: Death, Suffering, Change; (3) Foes and the Battle: Enemies of God and Man; (4) Guides and Helpers: Prophets, Shaykhs, and Saints; (5) Wings to Fly With: Fear, Hope, and Love; (6) Bitter and Sweet: Self-Discipline and Spiritual Progress; (7) Faith and Wisdom: The *Dīn* of Islam from Within; (8) Beyond Duality: Dilemmas Resolved; (9) Lord and Cherisher: The Relationship with God; (10) Aspects of Unity: Wisdom, Knowledge, Serenity. All translations in this *Treasury*, with two (acknowledged) exceptions, are by the compiler. Persian and Arabic words have been transliterated in Arabic style because it seems likely that more readers will have some familiarity with that language than with Dari Persian (also, the consonantal *wāw* was probably pronounced as *w* by the author and his contemporaries). The style of the *Treasury* series calls for the inclusion of the texts in the original language. In this case, however, it was decided to opt for a selection of them. The orthography of the

Persian texts has been simplified for the benefit of modern readers.

This *Treasury of Rūmī* represents, to borrow a Persian expression, 'a handful from the donkey-load' – a tiny sample of the immense spiritual riches to be found in the author's works. Innumerable passages of great beauty and profundity, and even many subject areas, have had to be left out. As for the commentaries, these are neither comprehensive nor faultless. For whatever is worthwhile in them the credit belongs to the compiler's teachers, to all of whom this little book is humbly dedicated. For whatever is defective, the fault is his alone. Despite its shortcomings, it is hoped that readers will find in this book a source of wisdom, consolation, and inspiration – and food for contemplation.

WHO ARE WE?
THE NATURE
AND DESTINY OF
MANKIND

Back to our Origins

Listen to this reed, how it tells its story
Complaining of the partings it has suffered.

'Ever since I was first cut from the reed-bed,
Men and women have moaned with my lamenting.

I need a bosom rent by parting's sorrow
In order to express the pain of longing.

For anyone left far away from his source
Misses the days when he was at one with it.

I've played my mournful notes in every gathering,
Consorting with the unhappy and the joyful.

All have become my friends – in *their* opinion;
But they've not sought out the secrets within me.

My secret's not far from my lamentation;
But ears and eyes have not the light to learn it.'

Body's not veiled from soul, nor soul from body;
But to see souls nobody has permission.

The cry of the reed-flute's not air, but fire.
May all who lack that fire come to nothing!

It is the fire of Love that's in the reed-flute;
What permeates wine is Love's fermentation.

The reed's a friend to those cut off from their Friend;
Its melodies tear down our veils, our ailments.

(M I, 1–11)

*A*lthough the format of the *Treasury* series necessitates that the selections be brief, it would be hard to do without the opening couplets of the *Mathnawī*, in which the poet presents the key themes of his masterpiece. These lines have been expounded by some distinguished authors, and the comments that follow contain little, if anything, that is original. Here one can only point to a few of the main points; readers may find further guidance in the works recommended in this book.

Mawlānā Rūmī begins the prose preface to *Daftar* (Volume) I of the *Mathnawī* in the normal manner, with the *Basmala* formula ('In the Name of Allah, the Infinitely Good, the Most Merciful'). The opening verses are unusual in that they begin instead with the word 'Listen' (or 'Hear': *Bishnaw*).

'This reed': a *nay* or stout reed is traditionally used in making two kinds of instruments of communication: pens and flutes. In either case a slit needs to be made at the front, for the passage of ink or of breathed air. The rending of garments is a gesture of grieving. (Music is a contentious matter among Muslims. Rūmī may have been, and his later successors certainly were, among those religious scholars who deemed the use of certain kinds of instrument lawful in spiritual gatherings.)

The reed laments being parted from its original home, and this echoes the human situation: in this world we are in exile from our true homeland in the Divine Presence. Very early in the history of the *Mathnawī*, copyists began to change 'this reed' to 'the reed', considering that an improvement; but the former is the correct reading and highlights the fact that the author is also speaking of himself and asking others to listen to his tale.

'May all who lack that fire come to nothing!' 'That fire' is the fire of love, and the fire of yearning for one's Beloved and one's home. What may sound like a most unfriendly imprecation is in fact a prayer for goodness for all: what prevents people from one having that love and longing is self-centredness, and the best thing that can happen to us is for our egos to be dissolved and 'come to nothing' in love for the Divine. This is how Rūmī introduces the key theme of his masterpiece.

2

Three Categories of Creatures

There are three categories of creatures. First there are the angels, who are pure intelligence. To be obedient, pious and constantly mindful of God is their nature, their sustenance. That is what they feed on and live by, like fish in the water whose life is through water and whose bed and pillow is the water. Angels are not subject to obligation. Being [purely] spiritual and free of appetite, what favour can they gain by abstaining from appetite or not experiencing carnal desires? Pure as they are, they do not have to struggle to avoid feeling passion. The acts of obedience [to God] they perform are not reckoned as such, since they are that way by nature and cannot be otherwise.

The second category is that of the beasts, which are [characterized by] unalloyed appetite and have no discriminatory intelligence. They too are not morally answerable. Not so the poor human being, [the third category]. He is a mixture of intellect and lust. Half of him is angel, half is animal; half is serpent, half fish. His fish pulls him towards water, his serpent towards dust;

they pull against one another constantly. He whose intellect subdues his lust is higher than the angels; he whose lust subdues his intellect is lower than the beasts.

> 'The angel is saved by his knowledge,
> the beast is saved by ignorance.
>
> Between those two, mankind's offspring
> are left to struggle with themselves.'

Some humans have followed their intellects so far as to become completely angelic, pure light. These are the Prophets and the *Awliyā'*, who are freed from [the limits of] fear or hope: '*Those who are not to be feared for, nor shall they sorrow*' (Qur'an 10: 62). There are others, however, who have been so far overcome by lust that they have become completely bestial. Others again remain struggling, being the group who display a certain pain or anguish and who are dissatisfied with their way of life. These are the believers. The *Awliyā'* stand waiting to bring them to their own [spiritual] station and make them like themselves. The devils, too, lie in wait, to pull them down to their own lowest level, the Abyss.

(FMF no. 17, 77–78; DOR 89–90; SOTU 81–82)

*T*his excerpt from one of Rūmī's discourses serves to set the scene for this *Treasury* by situating the Children of Adam in their place among the various orders of animate beings. We stand between the angelic beings and the animal kingdom, as do the jinn, the other of the two categories of creature known in Islam as 'the Two Weights' (*al-Thaqalān*). What we have in common are the responsibility that goes with the power to choose between good and evil, and the handicap of being 'a mixture of intellect and lust'. Yet but for these obstacles we could not merit any reward for obedience to God's commands. There is none for the angels, who are innately obedient and who have no appetite to be satisfied by tangible rewards.

When the Creator announced that He was establishing a Deputy on Earth, the angels anticipated that this meant the arrival of a creature who would cause trouble and bloodshed, and they were shocked. God then showed them the wisdom behind the creation of Adam, whose knowledge extended to knowing the 'names', or the inner realities, of all things. As for Adam's progeny, some (urged on by the *Awliyā'*, or saints) follow an upward path, some (urged on by the *Shayāṭīn*, or devils) a downward one. Others are believers who strive to maintain their faith and character – or rather to improve them, since it is practically very difficult to stand still in the conditions that face us. In practice, then, we are either progressing or regressing. Who will follow the upward Path?

3

The Human Microcosm

آدمی عظیم چیز است: در وی همه چیز مکتوب است.

حجب و ظلمات نمی گذارد

که او آن علم را در خود بخواند. حجب و ظلمات این

مشغولی های گوناگون است

وتدبیرهای گوناگون دنیا وآرزوهای گوناگون. با این

همه که در ظلمات است و

مـحجوب پرده هاست، هم چیزی میخواند و از

آن واقف است. بنگر که چون این

ظلمات و حجب بر خیزد، چه سان واقف گردد و از

خـود چه علم هـا پیدا کند. آخـر

این حـرفتها از درزیی وبنّایی ودروگـری

وزرگـری وعلم نجـوم

وطبُ وغیره وانواع حِرَف، الی ما لا یُعَدُّ وَ لَا یُحۡصَی

از اندرون آدمی پیدا شده است؛ از سنگ و کلوخ پیدا
نشد. آنکه میگویند زاغی
آدمی را تعلیم کرد که مرده در گور کند، آن هم عکس
آدمی بود که بر مرغ زد.
تقاضای آدمی اورا بر آن داشت. آخر حیوان جزو
آدمی است؛ جزو، کُلّ را چون آموزد؟

A human being is something vast; all things are inscribed within him. Yet veils and darknesses will not let him read the knowledge that he has inside him. The veils and darknesses are these various preoccupations, schemes, and worldly desires. Yet despite all these things being hidden in darknesses, concealed behind those veils, man is able to read something, and is aware of it. Consider how aware he becomes and what knowledge he discovers in himself when the darknesses and veils are removed. After all, trades like tailoring, building, carpentry, goldsmithing, science, astronomy, medicine, and so on – countless different trades – were discovered within mankind, not inside rocks or clods of earth. Now, it is said that a raven instructed man to bury the dead in a grave. That, too, was a reflection of human [intelligence] which came to the bird; it was an expression of human need that prompted him to do it. For animal [nature] is [merely] part of human [nature]. How could the partial teach the whole?
(FMF no. 11, 50; DOR 61–62; SOTU 52)

*T*owards the end of a fascinating discourse, Rūmī reminds us that the human soul contains universal knowledge. Despite appearances, every human being is a microcosm, a universe in miniature. The Qur'an tells us that the first man and Prophet, Adam (peace be upon him) was taught the names of all things. The name of anything, in primordial language, reflects its fundamental meaning and essential nature. Without the requisite knowledge present within them, how could the Children of Adam, at the beginning of their story, have testified to the Divine Lordship by themselves and on the basis of knowledge?

Mawlānā Rūmī cites the wide variety of trades and professions as examples of human knowledge and learned skills. One of the implications of this is that whatever may be the outward process involved, every kind of learning is a form of discovery (or what Greek sages called *anamnēsis*, 'unforgetting') within the soul. As enlightened educators often remark, the original meaning of 'education' is to bring something out. The privilege of being by *fiṭra* (primordial nature) *homo sapiens*, distinguished from other creatures by the modalities and extent of human knowledge, also carries responsibilities. God Most High swears by the human soul and its Creator that those who cultivate their souls will prosper and those who 'bury' them (beneath 'darknesses and veils') are doomed to utter failure.

4

The Believer's Heart

Compared to the vastness of [Adam's] pure soul,
the expanse of the seven heavens is narrow.

The Prophet related that God has said,
'I am not contained in the jar of "high" and "low";

I am not contained in earth or heaven, or even
Heaven's highest heights. Know this for sure, noble one.

Yet I am contained in the true believer's heart.
How wondrous! If you look for Me, search
in those hearts.'

(M I, 2652–2655)

*T*hese lines from the *Mathnawī* indicate the immensity
of the human soul with reference to a saying
sometimes cited as a *Ḥadīth Qudsī*, a Divinely
inspired Prophetic Tradition: 'Neither My heavens
nor My earth can contain Me, but the heart of My
believing servant contains Me.' This is an allusive
statement, not a literal one. God Almighty and

Majestic has no location or dimensions and cannot be contained in anyone or anything. The mind may understand something of God's Attributes (*ṣifāt*) but not His Ipseity or Essence (*dhāt*); and a hadith (Ṭabarānī, *al-Muʿjam al-awsaṭ*) forbids meditating on the latter, which could unbalance the mind. Yet the human heart, by virtue of its primordial nature, has the potential to become like a mirror reflecting the Divine Magnificence, 'embracing' It, so to speak, by a mode of direct, supra-rational, cognition (*maʿrifa*). As Mawlānā says (*Mathnawī* III, 2269):

> 'The heart is nothing other than that ocean
> of Light.
> It's the place where God is seen; how, then,
> could it be blind?'

The above explanation leaves some questions unanswered. Why, for instance, does the poet attribute these words to God: 'If you look for Me, search in those hearts'? Should not every seeker be searching within their own hearts? They should. But for those in need of guidance, the way to *begin* the search is to seek somebody qualified to help them; somebody whose heart already contains Divinely bestowed wisdom, knowledge, and *baraka* (blessing).

5

The Human Spirit

A bird flies in the atmosphere of the Unseen.
Its shadow falls on a patch of the Earth.

The body is the heart's shadow's shadow's shadow;
How could the body merit the heart's exalted rank?

A man lies asleep, his spirit shining in Heaven,
Like the sun, while his body is lying in bed.

His spirit is hidden in the Void, like a fringe
[inside a garment];
His body is tossing and turning beneath the blanket.

Since the spirit, being *from my Lord's Command*,
is invisible,
Any likeness I may pronounce belies the truth of it.
(M VI, 3306–3310)

O ne of the major themes of the final *Daftar* (Volume)
of the *Mathnawī* is the uniqueness of the human state.
In these lines Rūmī presents a series of arresting visual

images to evoke the distance and disparity between the bodily and spiritual aspects of the human being. The body is 'the shadow of the shadow of the shadow' of the heart, like a shadow cast on the Earth by the bird or the spirit as it flies in the realm of the Unseen. Asleep in his bed, a man tosses and turns, while far away his spirit shines in the heavenly realms. Citing Qur'an 17: 85, the poet reminds us that the spirit (*rūḥ*) is something beyond the reach of sense-perception. The Prophet, peace and blessings be upon him, was instructed to tell those who asked him about the spirit, that it is *min amr Rabbī*. This is generally translated, literally, as *'from my Lord's Command'* and is understood as signifying that the spirit is an entity whose nature is mysterious and fully known only to its Creator. According to the Qur'an, God 'blew' something of His spirit into our forefather, the Prophet Adam (peace be upon him); the attribution of the spirit to Him signifies not that it is divine but that it is among the most noble and wondrous of His creations.

The poet is not suggesting that the sleeping man is already living in Paradise while in this world. The message is that God causes the soul to pass away in its sleeping state, as Qur'an 39: 42 expresses it, then returns it to the body upon its awakening, unless He has decreed that it is to die. While mind and body are asleep the soul may roam the realm of the Unseen, whether confined to the domain of psychic phenomena and experiencing mundane or bizarre dreams or rising to the domain of spiritual 'unveilings'. Rūmī describes this in one of his poems (*Dīwān*, vol. 2, p. 229; ghazal 943):

> At the hour of the night prayer, when the sun has fully set,
> The senses' pathway closes; that of the Unseen opens.
>
> The angel in charge of sleep then starts driving spirits forward,
> The way that a shepherd does while watching over his flock,
>
> Beyond time and space, towards the pastures of the spirit;
> What cities and what gardens he shows to them over there!
>
> The spirit beholds a thousand amazing forms and people,
> When the imprint of this world is excised from it in dreams.
>
> You would say that the spirit had always dwelt in that world;
> It does not recall this world, or grow weary of that one.
>
> It feels so free from the burden and load that made its heart quake
> While here, that no such worries gnaw at him any longer.

Rūmī often speaks of sleep and dreams and their significance and connection with death. They are unmistakably signs and portents – aspects of the Unseen – that everyone experiences. And our real identities do not reside in our bodies:

> 'The body is the heart's shadow's shadow's shadow;
> How could the body merit the heart's exalted rank?'

6

The Real 'You'

You don't grasp that it is vital, although it is;
You too, in the end, will say: 'It was vital'.

He is *you* – not this 'you', but the [true] *you*
That is waiting and that will emerge in the end.

Your [true] *you* is buried inside something else.
I'm a slave to the man who can see his true self.

That which a young man can see in a mirror,
The spiritual guide can discern in a brick.

(M VI, 3774–3777)

*M*aking the journey to God while following a spiritual guide, who possesses profound insight (alluded to in the last couplet), is the means to discover one's true identity. The apparent 'you', the familiar one, is restricted to this three-dimensional world. You mistakenly suppose that to be the real 'you', but the reality of who *you* are is beyond those dimensions:

in the realm of the spirit. The familiar self we are accustomed to talking to and hearing from a thousand times daily is the one we must learn to manage, in keeping with the responsibility our Creator gave us in making us human. A 'brick' (*khisht*) here probably means a piece of metal of the kind from which mirrors were made.

What an extraordinary creation is the human soul, in which completely opposite attributes can co-exist! Its lower and worse side craves to have the satisfaction of having everything its own way, and fears change. On the other hand, its higher and better side longs for change and is ready to embrace it; it longs to transcend its apparent limits (precisely because it is a human, not an animal, soul). 'In its heart of hearts' the soul yearns for true and everlasting happiness and is always aware that there is a price to be paid and there are changes that have to be made. After all, that is a paltry price to pay for an immeasurable and everlasting blessing.

Several times in the Holy Qur'an God swears an oath, invariably by some object of exceptional significance. In *Sūrah al-Shams*, 'The Sun' (91: 8–9), He swears '*By the soul and that [Power] which formed it, then inspired it with its corruption (fujūr) or its God-consciousness (taqwā). He who grows it* (or purifies it, *zakkāhā*) *prospers; he who buries it* (or indulges it, *dassāhā*) *fails.*' So here lies the supreme challenge on the Path: one must go forwards, out of the 'comfort zone', or else risk losing everything. 'You don't grasp that it is vital, although it is; you too, in the end, will say: "It was vital."'

7

Don't Sell Yourself Short: The Value of the Human Being

حـقّ تعـالى تـرا قيمـت عظيـم كرده است. مى
فرمايد كه: [آية]:

إِنَّ ٱللَّهَ ٱشْتَرَىٰ مِنَ ٱلْمُؤْمِنِينَ أَنفُسَهُمْ وَأَمْوَٰلَهُم
بِأَنَّ لَهُمُ ٱلْجَنَّةَ ... ۞

[شعر]: تو به قيمت وراى دو جهانى
چه كنم قدر خود نمى دانى
مفـروش خويـش ارزان
كـه تـو بـس گـران بـهايى

حقّ تعالی می فرماید که: «من شمارا و اوقات و انفاس
شمارا و اموال و روزگار شمارا خریدم،
که اگر به من
صــرف رود و بــه مــن دهیــد، بهای آن بهشت جاویدانی
است. قیمت تو پیش من از این است.» اگر تو خودرا به
دوزخ فروشی، ظلم بر خود
کرده باشی، همچنان که آن مرد کارد صد دیناری را بر
دیوار زد و بر او.
کوزه ای یا کدویی آویخت.

God Most High has attached an immense price to you,
saying: *'God has purchased from the believers their
selves and their property, [pledging] that Paradise
shall be theirs'* (Qur'an 9: 111).

'In value you're beyond this world and the Next.
If you don't know your own worth, what can I do?'
(Sanā'ī, Ḥadīqat al-ḥaqīqa, p. 500, *bayt* 2)

'Don't sell yourself short; your value is immense.' God
Most High says: 'I have purchased you, your every
breath, your property, your lifespan. If they are spent on
Me and given to Me, their value is eternity in Paradise.
That is what you are worth to Me.' If you sell yourself to
Hell, you will have wronged yourself, like the man who
stuck a dagger worth a hundred [gold] dinars in the
wall and then hung a pot or gourd from it.
(FMF no. 4, 15; DOR 27–28; SOTU 17)

*T*o possess nobility, in any sense of the word, is a privilege granted by Providence – a Divine gift – which imposes obligations on the recipient. Since the Author of the Qur'an tells us (17: 70), '*We have ennobled the Children of Adam*', all humanity owes allegiance to the One from whom all gifts have come. Such is His generosity that He has undertaken to reward with eternal felicity those who sell Him their selves and their property – even though all of us and all our property already belong to Him – telling us, in effect, 'That is what you are worth to Me.' To refuse such an indescribably generous offer is ingratitude that brings terrible loss; but as Rūmī's great predecessor Sanā'ī expresses it, 'If you don't know your own worth, what am I to do?'

The 'you' whose value is in question here is the 'real you' of which Mawlānā speaks elsewhere in this book (M VI, 3774–3777). That 'real you' cannot be discovered without making sacrifices; and to sacrifice something is, literally, to consecrate it, to make it sacred. So our Creator calls on us to sacrifice something that is already rightfully His. The main value of the believer to their Lord and Cherisher lies in their heart. What else have we to offer to the One who has everything?

FACING FACTS:
DEATH, SUFFERING,
CHANGE

Death: This World is not our Home

You who have learned to wear a gold brocade robe
And belt, you'll end up in an unsewn garment!

We shall return to the earth from which we came.
Why have we fixed our hearts on transient creatures?

The Four Natures are our ancient ancestors, our kin,
So we have fixed our hopes on borrowed kinships.

For many long years, the body of mankind
Had close companionship with the elements.

Though Man's spirit belongs to the world of souls
And intellects, it has forsaken its roots.

From pure souls and intellects there comes a letter
To the spirit, which reads: 'O disloyal one,

You have found some miserable, five-day, friends –
And averted your face from your former friends.'

Children are happily engaged in playing,
[But] when night falls they're dragged off
and taken home.

At playtime the little child takes off his clothes;
A thief suddenly carries off his coat and shoes.

[The child] is so completely absorbed in playing
That his hat and his shoes are quite forgotten.

Night falls, and he cannot go on playing;
But now he does not have the nerve to go home.

Have you not heard that *'This life is naught but play'*?
You have squandered your goods and now you
are afraid.

Search for your clothing before the night comes;
Do not waste the daytime with [useless] talk.

(M VI, 446–458, 462)

*A*s seen in 'Three Categories of Creatures', humankind tends to be caught between its physical (or bestial) and its spiritual (or angelic) natures. Physically we are made of the four elements (earth, air, fire, and water), and the corresponding qualities of coldness, dryness, heat and moistness vie with each other in our physical and psychological makeup. 'For many long years, the body of mankind / had close companionship with the elements.' On the other hand, we are designed to aspire to purity and proximity to God. Yet many people who are aware that their true home is not in this world but in the Hereafter are subject to *ghafla* or heedlessness that can have a fatal impact on their lives. 'Though Man's spirit belongs to the world of souls / and intellects, it has forsaken its roots.' That is why it is important that the intelligence and spirit 'send a letter' to rebuke the forgetful for forsaking them in favour of their worldly attachments, their 'five-day friends'.

Sooner or later our fate in this world will be to exchange any fine clothes we may have for 'an unsewn garment': that is, a shroud. The theme of clothing is resumed at the end of this passage, in which the author uses another telling simile. A person who becomes absorbed in worldly desires and activities, forgetting about his true home, is likened to a child who continues happily playing outdoors until the sun has set. Having earlier taken off his hat and shoes to play, he belatedly finds that they have been stolen. Now it is too dark to go on playing, but he is afraid to go home without his hat and shoes. The poet asks, citing Qur'an 57: 20, 'Have you not heard that *"This life is naught but play"*?' Lastly he admonishes his audience to struggle against heedlessness and to prepare seriously for the Next Life:

> 'Search for your clothing before the night comes;
> Do not waste the daytime with [useless] talk.'

Why Must We Die?

A rejoinder to the simpleton who said 'This world would be fine were it not for death, and worldly wealth would be fine if it did not come to an end', and other absurdities of the kind.

That man used to say, 'This world would be fine,
If only death's foot were not planted in it.'

Said another, 'If there were no death at all,
The world would be worthless and tangled up,

A stack piled up in an empty field;
Abandoned, neglected and unthreshed.

You've imagined as life what is really death;
Sown your seed in salty, barren soil.

Truly, false reason views things inside-out:
it sees life as death, you weak-minded man.'

God, show us all things as they really are
In this abode where illusion is rife.

No dead person grieves on his death's account:
What he regrets is having too little in store.

Yet he's fallen from a pit out into the open
Amidst fortune, pleasure and relaxation.

From this abode of mourning, this narrow vale
He's been transported to the great outdoors –

'A Seat of Truth', not a palace of falsehood;
Choice wine, not being drunk with buttermilk.

The Seat of Truth, with God now his Companion:
He's escaped this water, the fire-temple's earth.

If you've not led the illuminative life,
There's a moment or two left: die like a man!
(M V, 1760–1772)

For the worldly-minded, and for what the poet calls a *mughaffal* – a heedless person or simpleton – this life may appear to be the be-all and end-all. The drawback is that neither possessions nor one's life here last for long. And that is just as well. For one thing, if all mankind and their possessions were to last forever, this world would be hopelessly cluttered with people and things, to an extent that is all too imaginable in today's world but was inconceivable in mediaeval times. By the Divine Wisdom, this world and all it contains is transitory. What is the use of lamentation, or of wishful thinking? We need (and should pray) to be enabled to see things as they truly are, not as we may wish them to be or as their supposed 'rationalism' leads the sceptic and the atheist to suppose.

Mawlānā warns us that 'false reason views things inside-out.' So it is that what appears to be death is in reality life. The real life is that of the Hereafter (Qur'an 29: 64), so abiding in this world forever would by no means be best for us. Although the dead had to leave this world behind, the major regret for most is not their departure itself but their awareness of 'having too little in store'; in other words, having failed to make adequate preparation and provision for their journey to Eternity by way of good deeds and beneficial knowledge. The concluding message from these lines brings us to a higher level. To find true life here, and to be forever in the highest position possible in the Hereafter, you must 'die to yourself' in this present life. Both the darker and the lighter side of existence are ultimately of greater value for those who resolve that duality. *Sub specie aeternitatis* (from the perspective of Eternity) whatever happens is for the best as Providence decreed.

Jalāl al-Dīn Rūmī resolves and dispels dualities with a degree of clarity that is rarely found elsewhere. The above lines offer a salient example, with their compelling final exhortation:

> 'If you've not led the illuminative life,
> There's a moment or two left: die like a man!'

3

God's Decree: People Are Answerable for their Actions

Said a thief to a magistrate, 'Your Honour,
The action I performed was decreed by God.'

'Well then, my friend,' the magistrate answered him,
'What I am doing is also decreed by God.'

If somebody steals a radish from a shop,
And says, 'O you wise man, this is God's decree,'

You'll punch his head twice or thrice, as if to say,
'O vile man, here is God's decree: put that back!'

You shameless wretch, such excuses aren't accepted
By greengrocers, even for one vegetable!

So why do you rely so much on that excuse,
And hang around such a dragon's neighbourhood?
(M V, 3058–3076)

*T*he dialogue in this passage is a fine example of the use of humour for didactic purposes. It is set in a courtroom; but in the setting of daily life, too, we may find ourselves putting forward in our own minds arguments and excuses that resemble the one put forward by the thief. If we did something wrong it was not our fault: it was just the way that things turned out, and it could not have been otherwise. The response is that although it is true that as Qur'an 37: 96 states, '*God created you and that which you do*,' we are nevertheless answerable for our own wrongdoing, except in circumstances where we genuinely can say we have no choice or are really acting under compulsion. Experientially, people know that normally they have a choice between performing an action and desisting from it.

One should not be deluded into thinking that if the offence seems slight – like the theft of one radish – it does not really matter. It is not excusable. The 'dragon' whose neighbourhood we are urged to avoid is a real danger: complacency, arising from heedlessness of the fact that God is aware of our every action. If we choose to do the wrong thing, sooner or later Divine punishment can be expected to follow, unless we repent and our repentance is accepted.

4

Illusion and the Causator of Causes

تو ز طفلی چون سبب ها دیده ای

در سبب، از جهل، بر چفس۔یده ای

با سبب ها، از مُسبِّبْ غافلی

سوی این رو پوش ها ز ان مایلی

چون سبب ها رفت، بر سر می زنی

رَبَّنَا و رَبَّنَا هــا می کنــی.

Having looked to apparent causes since you
were an infant,
Through ignorance you've grown attached to
each apparent cause.

Being distracted by these causes makes you
neglect the Causator;
That's the reason why you're so obsessed
with those veils.

When all apparent causes vanish, you'll beat your head
And cry out many times, '*O our Lord! O our Lord!*'
(M III, 3153–3155)

*M*ost people are accustomed from childhood to
interacting within the world as though all things were
the product or result of independent causes. In reality,
however, these are mere contingent possibilities which
veil The Reality. Their causation is entirely subject
to the control of God, the Lord and Cherisher of the
Universe (*Rabb al-ʿĀlamīn*), every particle of which
is determined in accordance with His perfect and
unfathomable wisdom, its destiny contained in His
timeless, infinite and perfect knowledge. One should
pray, as did the Blessed Prophet himself, 'Lord, show
me things as they truly are!'

From the everyday practical viewpoint, of course,
one has normally to approach matters from the
perspective of causation: for example, by turning on
the tap to get water – if the tap, and more importantly
the water, are there. At the same time, we need to
bear in mind always that not a single drop of water
can ever flow, for us or for any another creature,
without the permission of the *Musabbib al-Asbāb*, the
Causator of Causes (cf. Qur'an 67: 30). To overlook
this is to risk one day 'beating one's head and crying
out' – perhaps too late! As God's servants, it ought
to be our invariable practice to petition our Lord
for every need, however apparently trivial; for '*You*

alone do we worship, and Your help alone do we seek' (*iyyāka naᶜbudu wa iyyāka nastaᶜīn*: Qur'an 1: 5). If our request is granted, we also have the merit of having pleased Him by asking. If it appears not to be granted, it must be remembered that our Generous Creator never refuses those who ask, unless they have condemned themselves to refusal through some major sin for which they have not repented.

So if the request is not granted straight away, one of three things will happen instead. Either the thing we pray for or else something that God knows to be better for us will be granted later, and meanwhile there is a chance to earn merit by showing trust and patience; or instead of receiving it we will be spared from some evil thing that would otherwise have befallen us; or, alternatively, what we sought will be granted not in this world but in the Next, in which case it will come, God willing, in so splendid and perfect a form that people may even wish that none of their petitions had been granted in this lower world, whose lowly and transient nature will then be clear to see.

As the recipients of such incalculable and unmerited generosity and kindness, we must never fail to express our gratitude to the Causator, the Bestower of All, in both word and deed. As He reminds us collectively in the Qur'an (16: 53), *'Whatever blessings you may have, they are from God;'* and as He promises us (Qur'an 14: 7), *'If you give thanks I will certainly give you increase.'*

5

Everyone Has their Qibla

The Ka'ba of Gabriel and the celestial spirits
is a Lote-tree;
The glutton's *qibla* is a cloth laden with dishes of food.

The *qibla* of the '*ārif* is the light of union with God;
the *qibla* of the philosopher's mind is fantasy.

The *qibla* of the ascetic is God, the Gracious;
the *qibla* of the flatterer is a purse of gold.

The *qibla* of the spiritual is patience and long-suffering;
the *qiblah* of form-worshippers is an image of stone.

The *qibla* of those who live in the inward
is the Bounteous One;
the *qibla* of those who worship the outward
is a woman's face.

(M I, 1896–1900)

*I*t takes all kinds to make a world.' Humans having been created to know and serve God, even in their most debased condition, they still tend to have some sense of, and need for, the Absolute, even if it may be a misguided and perverted one. Deflected from the true Absolute through pride, misguidance, stubbornness, and hardness of heart, they orient their lives and their deepest attachment to something else. In this passage the poet draws a telling contrast between those enlightened by Divine Guidance on the Straight Path and those who are the object of Divine Anger and those who are misguided.

Some of the contrasted pairs in this passage are worth noting. Who does Mawlānā contrast with the ʿārif bi-Lllāh, someone with direct experiential knowledge of God? Not someone who takes everything in the world at face value, and who attaches excessive importance to worldly concerns, but someone who 'lives in his head', so to speak: the philosopher, whose mental operations and machinations are founded on, and end in, illusions. It is important to bear in mind that Rūmī was not against rational intellectual activity as such; almost certainly this criticism is directed at philosophers with secularist or even heretical tendencies, such as those who believed the world to be eternal. In any case, Mawlānā teaches insistently that it is light and knowledge in the heart that count for most.

In another *bayt* (couplet) we find that in contrast with materialist idol-worshippers, the *qibla* of spiritually-centred people is patience and long-suffering. Logically speaking, you might expect these qualities to be described as a means to an end, rather than as a *qibla*, an orientation or a goal to aim for. Perhaps the reason for putting them as an objective here was to emphasize that sincerity in the spiritual path involves making oneself pleasing to the Divine Beloved rather than aiming to gain anything from Him. Patience and endurance are acts of the heart which are dear to Him, Exalted is He; and to make one's main aim the acquisition of such attributes rather than gaining Paradise is a mark of sincerity and *ʿubūdiyya*, total servanthood.

Lastly, the contrast drawn between people of the inward and people of the outward does not mean there is no place for the love of a woman's (or a man's) face in the spiritual life. But if one's *qibla* is the Divine Entity Itself, human beauty is to be viewed in its appropriate place as a manifestation of God's Perfect and Unlimited Creativity and His concern for the happiness of His creation. That way, once we are established in that way of perceiving things, our human loved ones will not become less beloved to us, but more. '*And whatever bounties are yours, they are from God*' (Qur'an 16: 53).

6

No Gain Without Pain

Now hear this tale from a true narrator
Of the customs and ways of the men of Qazwīn.

Unflinching, they get themselves tattooed
With a needle-point, on body, arms and shoulders.

To the tattooist went a man of Qazwīn,
Saying 'Tattoo me. Make it a real beauty.'

'What design would you like, champ?'
the artist enquired.
'Do me a fierce lion!' the customer said.

'Leo's my ascendant, so draw me a lion.
Do your utmost, and pencil it dark and bold.'

'Where shall I draw this figure?' the tattooist asked.
'Put that lion on my shoulder-blade,' the other replied.

The tattooist started pressing his needle in,
And his customer's shoulder was racked with pain.

Our hero began wailing, 'Distinguished sir,
You're killing me! What is that you are drawing?'

The tattooist said, 'A lion is what you ordered.'
'What part did you start with?' the customer asked.

'I began with the tail-end,' the artist replied.
'Leave the tail out, dear friend!' the champion said.

'Tail and tail-end have knocked the breath out of me.
The lion's tail has got a hold on my windpipe.

Lion-smith, tell the lion to be tail-less,
For my heart is faint from the blows of that spike.'

The tattooist started etching in a different spot,
Without any care or caution or compunction.

The man yelled out, 'What part is this now?'
'My good sir, it's the ear,' the tattooist replied.

'Then let it be ear-less, Doctor!' said the man.
'Forget the ears and keep the picture simple.'

So the tattooing started in another place,
But the man of Qazwīn began bawling again.

'What's this third part that you're working on?'
'This is the belly of the lion, illustrious sir.'

'Let the lion do without a belly' said the champ.
'Cut the needlework down, for the pain is too much!'

The tattooist, flummoxed, was now at a loss.
For a long while his fingers remained in his mouth.

Then, enraged, the artist threw his pen to the ground,
And exclaimed: 'Has anyone in the world suffered this?

Who ever saw a lion with no tail, head or belly?
God Himself has never created such a lion!'

Brother, brave the pain of the lancet to escape
The poison in your fire-worshipping self;

For the sky, the sun, and the moon bow down
Before those who've escaped from self-centred existence.

(M I, 2981–3003)

Owing to the format of the *Treasury* series it has only
been possible to include one full-length story from
the *Mathnawī*, and here it is. The moral of the tale
is clear and is summarized in the heading. (Note that
tattooing is not permitted by Islamic law; but what
it stands for here is self-improvement, which for the
'he-man' of Qazwīn, a city in northwest Iran, took
that particular form. In Persian, putting a finger
to your mouth signifies amazement, bafflement, or
despair.)

Some modern Rūmī interpreters present him as a
proponent of the notion that 'I'm OK, you're OK';
also, verses such as the oft-quoted lines beginning
'Come again, come again' have been wrongly
attributed to him. He would certainly have agreed
with the actual author of those lines that 'this court
of ours is not the court of despair,' for the door of
repentance is open to all; but that is not the keynote
of his teachings. If one had to summarize Rūmī's
message in one sentence, something like this might

be closer to the mark:'If you truly desire everlasting happiness, give your love to God and trust in Him, and leave your comfort zone behind!'

Why Trials Come
our Way

How much hardship our minds endure, that we
may strain from dregs what's pure!
The trials of winter and autumn, summer heat,
spirit-like spring;

The winds, and clouds, and lightning-bolts.
All these things manifest contrasts,
To make the dusty earth bring out what its
chest holds – rubies or stones,

All this dark earth has stolen from God's
Treasury, Seas of Largesse.
Jail-Governor Fate says, 'Tell the truth: own up
what you took, hair by hair.'

That thief, the Earth, says 'Nothing! Zilch!'
The Governor then starts grilling it:
First speaking sweet, kind words to it, then
doing his worst, hanging it up –

So that, between 'soft and hard cop', Fear and
Hope's fire brings all to light.
Spring is the Almighty Governor's grace; Autumn,
God's menace and His threat,

Winter, symbolic crucifixion to expose you,
hidden thief.
The warrior's heart is sometimes glad, sometimes
oppressed, tormented, pained.

This clay and water – our bodies – deny and
steal our spirits' light.
Brave man, our Lord subjects our frames to
heat and cold, to woe and pain,

Fear, hunger, weakness, poverty, to 'see the
colour of our money.'
He's issued threats and promises because of
this mixed good and ill;

Truth and falsehood have been mixed up, real and
forged coins thrown in one purse.
A chosen touchstone is required, tried and tested
on seeming truths,

to show the false for what it is, and endorse
acts of Providence.
Mother of Moses, feed and cast him in the
water. Fear no trial!

Whoever drank that milk upon the Day of
the First Covenant
Will recognize the milk, as [the infant] Moses
[knew his mother's].

If you desire that your child[-soul] learn
how [thus] to discriminate,
Then you must suckle him, O you who are
'mother to a Moses';

So he may recognize the taste of the milk that
his mother gives,
And he may never bow his head to [drink milk
from] an evil nurse.

(M II, 2950–2972)

This passage from *Daftar* (Volume) II of the *Mathnawī* contains the author's wisdom on several subjects in a few lines. He begins by evoking the strains and stresses that life's vicissitudes impose – not on our hearts, as one might expect him to say, but on our minds. The struggle to make sense of it all and to come out on top, spiritually speaking, is like trying to strain a pure liquid out of dregs or leftovers. This world subjects us to endless changes and tests, for our Lord and Creator 'to see the colour of our money.' Experiencing and dealing with them provides countless opportunities to learn to be patient and to distinguish truth from falsehood. To apply criteria by which to do so, the poet explains, is innate to every human being. When we acknowledged the Divine Lordship in the Presence of God, on the Day of *Alast*, we drank the milk of true wisdom – wisdom that is part of the *fiṭra*, the primordial nature, of *homo sapiens*. When the Prophet, peace and blessings be upon him, was offered wine, water or milk to drink and he chose milk, he was told by the Archangel Gabriel (peace be upon him) that this was the best choice since it represented the *fiṭra*.

The Qur'an (20: 37–40) relates how the mother of Moses, to save him from being slaughtered by Pharaoh's men along with other Jewish infant boys, was ordered by God to cast him into the River Nile. Carried along in a box or basket, he was picked out of the water. As God had promised, and thanks to his sister's intervention, the baby was returned to his mother for suckling, having refused to drink the milk of any woman but his own mother. This, together with events in his adult life – see, for example, the Qur'anic narratives in *Sūrah Ṭā Hā* (20) and also in *al-Qaṣaṣ* (28) – illustrate the many ways in which God took care of him (*'And I have attached you to Me'*: 20: 41) through some extraordinary ups and downs. Moses, peace and blessings be upon him, is one of the greatest of God's chosen Emissaries; but we should never forget that Divine Concern is watching over every one of us at every moment, closer than the jugular vein – and that in the end, as is affirmed in a *Ḥadīth Qudsī*, He will deal with us according to our expectations of Him: 'I am as My servant thinks Me to be' (Bukhārī, *Ṣaḥīḥ*). Why should we not expect goodness from the One to whom we owe everything we have, and who provides food and shelter even to those who deny His existence?

8

The Proof of True Love

عشـق چـون دعـوی، جفـا دیدن گـواه؛

چـون گـواهـت نیسـت، شد دعوی تباه

چون گواهت خواهد این قاضی، مرنج

بـوسـه ده بـر مـار تـا یـابی تـو گنج

ایـن جفـا بـا تو نبـاشـد، ای پسـر

بـلک بـا وصـــفِ بَدی انـدر تـو در

Love's like a lawsuit: to suffer harshness is proof.
If you possess no evidence, your case is lost.

When this Judge demands evidence, don't be aggrieved.
Kiss the serpent, so that you may gain the treasure.

This harshness, my lad, is not at your expense:
It's directed towards the evil traits in you.

(M III, 4009–4010)

*T*hese four couplets teach several points with concision and eloquence. Firstly, God does not put us through tests in this life merely for His own amusement – 'this harshness … is not at your expense' – but in order to give us the opportunity to overcome the passivity, cowardice and meanness that are part of human nature at its worst. The challenge facing all human beings is this: to show our faith in Him through our trust and patience. In the ancient, timeless, myths of many peoples, a hero must confront great dangers to win the object of his quest. The more precious the treasure, the more formidable the dragon that guards it. As for the priceless and eternal treasure of bliss in the Hereafter, Divine Justice demands that there be obstacles for us to overcome in order to begin to merit it; in reality, however, the price to be paid is infinitesimally small in relation to the value of the reward. The truly devoted and thankful servant will gladly embrace the challenge, without being aggrieved, and will 'kiss the dragon'. That is the sign of sincerity, without which our actions amount to nothing. If we fail to produce adequate evidence of our devotion, in the end our case will be lost: our claim to love our Divine Lord will be shown up as false and will be rejected.

9

Commitment: A Matter of Love and Death

چه بی وفا جانی که بر ذوُ اَلوفا عاشـق نشـد!

قهرِ خدا باشد کـه بر لطفِ خدا عاشـق نشـد

چون کرد بر عالم گذر سلطان «مَـا زاَغَ الْبَصَـرْ»

نقشی بدید آخر که او بر نقش ها عاشـق نشـد

جانی کجا باشد که او بر اصلِ جان مفتون نشد؟

آهـن کجـا باشـد که بر آهنْ ربا عاشـق نشـد؟

مـن بـر در این شـهرْ دِی بَشْـنیدم از جمعِ پری:

«خانهْ ش بده، بادا که او بر شهرِ ما عاشق نشد!»

ای وای آن ماهی که او پیوسته بر خشـکی فتد؛

ای وای آن مسّی که او بـر کیمیـا عاشـق نشـد!

بسـته بُوَد راهِ اجل، نَبْوَد خـلاصش مُعْتَجَل؛
هم عیش را لایق نَبُد، هم مرگ را عاشق نشد.

How faithless is the soul that's not in love with
the Most Faithful One!
The Wrath of God be upon the one who has
not fallen for God's Grace.

When that monarch *'whose sight strayed not'*
journeyed beyond the entire world,
Not being in thrall to outer form, he saw a
Form beyond all forms.

Where is there a soul that is not in love
with all souls' Origin?
Where is the iron that is not in love with
the Magnetic One?

Beside the city gate last night I heard a band
of fairies (*parī*) say:
'Find him a dwelling; God forbid that he fall
in love with our town!'

How sad is the fate of a fish that keeps
falling upon dry land!
How sad the fate of copper that is not in
love with the Elixir!

The way's blocked to his dying hour;
there is no quick escape for him.
He is not fit to be alive, nor has he fallen
in love with Death.

(D II, 1; ghazal 523)

*T*he central theme of these lines is that it is part of original sound human nature (*fiṭra*) to feel a stronger attachment to the Creator than to anyone or anything else. It is also part of *fiṭra* nature to aspire to refine oneself by transcending one's limitations. God's 'faithfulness' is His constant compassion and concern for His creatures – even for those who show no reverence and/or deny Him; and also His generosity to those who are dutiful towards Him. Those who are not strongly attached to the Lord and Cherisher who provides for all their needs, says Rūmī, are neither 'fit to be alive' nor 'in love with Death' as are those who long to meet their Lord. They are like fish out of water, and are looked upon with aversion by the pure-hearted (the local 'band of fairies'). Amongst those 'in love with Death' are the people who strive to follow the example of the Prophet, upon whom be blessings and peace, whose '*sight strayed not*' (Qur'an 53: 17) but remained fixed upon God Himself even when he passed miraculously, in his bodily frame, from the confines of this lower world into the realms beyond, where he beheld 'a Form beyond all forms'. Although he alone was granted that privilege while still alive in this world, the most fortunate of believers are permitted to experience for themselves a divine attraction which 'magnetizes' them permanently, and perhaps even the direct cognition of God which is like an elixir that turns hearts to gold.

FOES AND THE
BATTLE: ENEMIES OF
GOD AND MAN

1

The World of Opposites

When you look at it, this entire world is a battle,
Atom fighting atom, like faith and unbelief.

One particle goes flying off to the left;
Another goes off to the right, in its search.

One atom's above and the other below;
See how in the elements their actions clash.

But a particle that's blotted out by the sun
Has no conflict left to be counted or described.

When an atom has lost both its self and its breath,
No conflict remains except that of the sun.

Its natural movement and stillness are gone.
Why? Because '*We are God's, and to Him we return.*'

From ourselves we've returned to that Ocean of Yours,
Weaned away from the breast milk of our origins.

You whom ghouls have left stuck where the
pathways divide,
Unprincipled one, don't speak of principles!

When seen in their true light, our war and our peace
Come not from us but from '*between Fingers twain*'.

Conflict between natures and actions and words –
There's a terrible war between conflicting parts.

Yet by that very conflict this world is sustained;
Analyse this by looking at the elements.

Four mighty pillars are the four elements,
Rising to the level of the roof of the world.

Each element is the downfall of another:
The element of Water puts out Fire's sparks.

All creation, then, is based upon opposites,
So we are bound to fight over profit and loss.

The Next World is abundant and everlasting,
Because it is not made up of opposites.

* *

Why is it, good sir, that we're such contraries?
From all these numbers how can unity spring?

We are branches; the four opposites are their roots.
It's the root that gave every branch its own traits.

The essence of the spirit transcends all divisions:
its nature reflects the Divine Transcendence.

(M VI, 36–50, 61–63)

awlānā Rūmī frequently reminds his readers and listeners of this world's deficiencies. Its transitory nature is unsurprising – '*We are God's, and to Him we return*' (Qur'an 2: 156) – considering the opposing forces at work in it. Its physical foundations, after all, are the four natural elements (in Persian and Arabic these are called *arkān*, pillars) which both intrinsically and symbolically represent the fundamental oppositions inherent in the world of phenomena. At the same time, these elements are complementary; and without them the physical universe would not exist.

In the Next World, for the blessed the complementary nature of things prevails over the conflicts; for those condemned to Hell, the conflicts prevail over the complementary. There is no counterpart to Hell-Fire that can lessen it, unless the Divine Compassion intervenes: '*their torment shall not be lightened*' (Qur'an 2: 86, 2: 162, and 3: 88). But God knows best, and He is the Most Compassionate. '*Fingers Twain*' alludes to a Tradition (Muslim, *Ṣaḥīḥ*) according to which the hearts of all Adam's Children are, metaphorically speaking, held between two Fingers of God: these are interpreted as being His *Jalāl* (Majesty and Severity) and His *Jamāl* (Beauty and Kindness).

Traditional Muslim physicians, following the ancient Hellenic (*Yūnānī*) tradition, seek to restore their patients to health by re-establishing the equilibrium between the four 'humours' in their constitution, which are hot, cold, moist, or dry. The human soul, too, is subject to internal conflict requiring treatment by a spiritual physician and striving on the Path, until its constituent elements are restored to the complete equilibrium which characterizes its *fiṭra* or primordial nature. The purity thus acquired (or regained) is that of 'the essence of the pure spirit', which 'transcends all divisions: its nature reflects the Divine Transcendence.'

2

The Animal Soul

The animal soul's kept alive by food;
Be its state good or bad, it dies all the same.

If this lamp dies and it goes out, why then
Should the neighbour's house become dark as well?

Since without this lamp there's still light in that house,
Each home has a different sense-perception lamp.

That likeness applies to the animal soul;
It is not a likeness of the God-guided soul.

(M IV, 453–456)

*H*ere Jalāl al-Dīn Rūmī contrasts the animal soul with the human soul. Each has its own individual destiny, a unique modality of potential 'God-guidedness'. Human souls possess an aspect of animal nature, which conforms to animal instincts; but they also have an aspect of angelic nature, which aspires to higher levels of being. Human consciousness has been created for the eternal life which shall be ours, for good or ill, after bodily death and resurrection. When death comes, our animal soul perishes ('this lamp dies and it goes out'); but in 'the neighbour's house', as the poet puts it, the lamp of the spirit lives on although the lamp of physical life and perception has ceased to burn.

The precious *rūḥ* or Spirit is an imperishable entity, destined for eternal life in either ineffable bliss or unimaginable misery. Failure to live up to the elevated nature of our human state is a form of *kufr*, a word that can mean covering up the truth, or ingratitude, or unbelief. Not to take advantage of such an immense privilege is a betrayal of the sacred *amāna* or Trust, which all humankind consented to bear on the Day of *Alast*, when our spirits bore witness to the Divine Lordship (Qur'an 7: 172). So while the existence of appetites in humankind is necessary and ordained by Divine Wisdom, our ego in its animal aspects is an enemy to the fulfilment of our mission.

3

Subduing the Self

O kings, we have killed the outward enemy,
but within us remains a worse enemy than him.

Slaying this foe is not a task for reason and intelligence:
The lion within cannot be overcome by a hare.

This ego is Hell, and Hell is a dragon
Whose fire cannot be quenched by oceans of water.

It could drink up the Seven Seas, yet still the fire
Of that creature-devourer would not become less.
(M I, 1373–1376)

*I*n Sufi literature we often read that vanquishing external enemies is easier than subduing one's own demons. The ego (*nafs*) is powerful, devious, resourceful and persistent. Attempts to overcome such an adversary by means of mental operations are unlikely to succeed. If confronted with a dragon, the poet tells us, one must 'fight fire with fire'. The sources testify that many Sufi masters subjected themselves and their disciples to forms of self-mortification more rigorous than most of us can picture ourselves surviving, much less prospering on. Mawlānā Jalāl al-Dīn was himself a highly accomplished *zāhid* or ascetic.

Today, however, people are generally far less robust and the emphasis is more often on training the self more gently and 'diplomatically', by keeping its desires from excessive indulgence and exercising them strictly within the bounds of Sacred Law: 'fighting fire with water', so to speak. There is a risk that the self, if subjected to more pressure than it can handle, may rebel and lead its owner into a potentially disastrous state of imbalance.

Why is it that reasoning alone is normally ineffectual in subduing the domineering tendencies of *al-nafs al-ammāra*, the imperious self? The mind tends to resort to reason to justify any desires that arise and to prompt one to gratify them. It is therefore necessary to have recourse to a higher faculty to cut off or, better, prevent this process. That faculty is the heart, which can be purified by the remembrance of God and by keeping company with the pure-hearted, preferably in person, but alternatively by reading or listening to their words. Try this and see. If you sit with people for whom the *dunyā*, this world, is their overwhelming concern, this world and its concerns will probably start to fill your mind and the Next World and the life of the spirit will seem to shrink right down. Sit with people whose overwhelming concern is their spiritual life and the Next Life, and you will experience the opposite. *'Be ever conscious of God, and be with the sincere'* (Qur'an 9: 119).

In the first line, the poet says 'O kings …' He is addressing those who are devoted to the Sufi Path, of whom it is often said that they are inwardly kings – whatever their social status and outward condition – whereas devotees of worldly life are poor in that they never feel they have enough.

4

Inward Impurity

Outward filth may be removed with some water,
But inward filthiness steadily grows.

It cannot be washed away except with tears,
Once the filth that's inside has become manifest.

God has called the unbeliever 'impure';
that impurity's not in his outward being.

The unbeliever is not defiled by outward impurity;
That impurity is in his nature and religion.

Outward impurity's smell spreads for twenty paces;
Inward impurity's stench spreads from
Rayy to Damascus.

(M III, 2092–2096)

*F*or those who see things as they truly are, the impurity
of evil actions, thoughts and deeds is far, far more
disgusting than outward impurity, even though
avoiding and eliminating external impurity is of great

importance to Muslims. Ritual purity (*ṭahāra*) is an essential condition for the legal validity of prayers. In most works on *fiqh* (jurisprudence), the opening sections are devoted to the rulings on purity and discuss the various forms of *najāsa* or impurity and how to eliminate them.

Inward impurity, by comparison, is more insidious and harder to deal with. Commenting on his paraphrase of part of Qur'an 9: 28, Rūmī teaches that the crucial impurity in the inveterate polytheists (the term used in the Scripture being *mushrikūn*) – he means those who deny faith not out of ignorance but in the face of clear truth – is not their lack of ritual or physical cleanliness but their inward impurity. In saying that inward impurity grows, he means that unless one becomes aware of one's faults or vices and makes up one's mind to remedy them, it is likely that these evils will increase. (The city of Rayy was in part of what is now southern Tehran.) The key to cleansing this kind of deadly impurity is sincere repentance, for 'it cannot be washed away except with tears.'

5

Heedlessness: Forgetting our Homeland

The ego is Pharaoh's follower: beware, don't satisfy it,
Lest it recall its long-time infidelity.

Without the glowing heat of the fire [of training]
The lower self will never become goodly.

Pay attention, don't beat upon the iron
Until it has become [red hot] like live coals.

Without hunger the body will not move [towards God].
Be aware that it's cold iron that you are beating!

Though it may weep and lament most pitifully,
It will never become a believer. Take heed!

Like Pharaoh, during famine it bows before Moses,
As did [Pharaoh], while making supplication;

[But] once it has been freed from want, it will rebel:
When the donkey has cast off his load, he will kick.

So, when its business has gone well, [the ego]
Forgets its sighs and its lamentations.

If a man who lives in a city [for] years,
As soon as his eyes have gone to sleep,

Sees another city full of good and evil,
His own city won't come to his memory at all,

That [he should say], 'I have lived there [so long].
This new city is not mine: here I am [just] in pawn.'

No, he thinks that truly he has always lived
In that very city, and was born and bred there.

What wonder [then] if the soul does not remember
Its [old] haunts, its former home and birth-place?

Since this world, like sleep, covers it all up
The way that the clouds cover over the stars;

Especially as it has trodden so many cities,
And the dust has not been swept from its
sense-perceptions.

Nor has it striven hard so that its heart
Should become pure and behold the past,

And put out its head through the mystery's opening
And see end and beginning with open eyes.

(M IV, 3621–3636)

As this and other passages in the *Treasury* show, Mawlānā Rūmī is far from being the kind of teacher who tells us 'Everything's OK.' On the contrary, he repeatedly describes the wiles and the dangers of the *nafs*, the ego. Here we are warned of two of its chief characteristics. Firstly, like the Pharaoh of the Prophet Moses' time it considers itself the be-all and end-all, before whom all should bow. Secondly, even when subjected to discipline and training, the *nafs* is obstinate and determined; unless put under constant pressure it will always try to kick back and have its own way.

Mawlānā enriches his description of the habits and wiles of the *nafs* with a telling simile. The believer's heart and mind remember and learn from experience, but the ego tends to revert blindly to its old ways at the first opportunity, turning its back on its 'home town' as soon as it catches a glimpse of a new and alluring 'city' that appears to offer fresh delights. Such attractions make it prone to forget its transient nature and all the disappointments and frustrations of worldly life. 'What wonder [then] if the soul does not remember / its [old] haunts, its former home and birth-place?' It is the *nafs* – with its desires and delusions – that leads us to forget that our true home is not in this world but in proximity to our Lord and Creator: that is, in Paradise. Only by overcoming the ego can hearts be purified so that they behold Reality and 'see end and beginning with open eyes.'

6

This Deceptive World

The property, wealth and satin of this [worldly] journey
  Are chains that hold back the swift-moving soul.

Seeing a chain of gold, it has been taken in.
  The soul's not in the open but stuck down a pit –

Which appears like heaven but is really a hell:
  A lethal snake dressed as a rosy-cheeked [girl].

You imperfect ones, beware of this rose-cheeked beauty;
  Keep her company, and she'll emerge as hellish!'
                    (M VI, 243–246)

*M*ight this be the very darkest of all Rūmī's characterizations of this deceptive world and its deceptions? Life is a journey: we pass through this world, and no wealth or possessions can be ours for more than a short while. Yet people are easily ensnared by the chains of gold, property and luxury. These chains hold back the soul, which ought to be moving swiftly

and progressing constantly along the path away from
worldly illusions and towards the true Reality. As the
Prophet, peace and blessings be upon him, observed:
'This world is a prison to the believer, a paradise to
the unbeliever' (Muslim, *Ṣaḥīḥ*). While the deceived
soul believes itself to be out in a congenial open space,
it is in fact 'stuck down a pit – which appears like
heaven but is really a hell … a lethal snake' disguised
as a beautiful woman. Those of us who are 'imper-
fect', and have yet to reach the station of seeing things
as they are, must beware.

Why, apart from playing on words, does Mawlānā
speak of the soul (*rawān*) here as 'swift-moving'
(*rawān*)? Because we need always to be conscious
that our life on Earth is not a static experience but
a journey. However hard we may try to keep things
just as they are, we will learn sooner or later that the
world just does not allow that.

7

The Envious Enemy

زِ روی نـخـوت و تـقـلـیـد، نـنگ دارد از او
بُلیسْ وار، که خود بـس بُـوَد خـدا مسـجـود
جواب گویدش آدم که «این سجود اوراست
تو احولی و دو می بینی از ضلال و جحود.»
زِ گَـردِ چـون و چـرا پـرده ای فـرود آورد
میـانِ اخـترِ دولـت، میـانِ چشـمِ حسـود.
سـتـاره گـویـد: «رَو. پـرده تـو افـزون بـاد
ز من نـمانـدی تنهـا، ز حضـرتی مـردود.»
بسـا سؤال و جـوابی کـه انـدر ایـن پرده سـت
بـدیـن حـجـاب نـدیـدی خـلیل را نمـرود؟
چه پرده است حسد، ای خـدا، میـان دو یـار
که دِی چو جان بُده اند، این زمان چو گرگْ عنود

چـه پـرده بـود، کـه ابلیـس پیـش از ایـن پـرده

بـه سـجده، بام سـمَوات و ارض مـی پیمـود!

بـه رغبت و بـه نشـاط و بـه رقّـت و بـه نیـاز

بـه گـونه گـونه مناجـات مـهر مـی افـزود.

ز پـرده حسـدی مانْـد همـچو خـر بـر یـخ

کـه آن همـه، پر و بالـش بدیـن حـدث آلـود.

ز مسجد فلکش رانْد: «رَو، حـدثی کردی!»

حـدیث مـی نشـنود، و حـدث مـی پالـود.

«چـراروم؟ چه حجّت؟ چه کرده ام؟ چه سبب؟

بیـا کـه بحـث کنیـم، ای خـدایِ فـردِ ودود!

اگر بَد است تو کردی، کـه جملـهٔ کرده تست:

ضـلالتِ وثنـی و مسیحیـان و جـهـود.

مـرا چو گُمْرَه کـردی، مـرادِ تـو ایـن بـود

چنان کـنم که نبیـنی ز خـلق یک مـحمود.»

This one is like Iblīs: from pride and conformity
he disdains
[To acclaim] him. He says, 'God is enough for me
to prostrate to.'

Adam replies to him, 'This prostration's intended
for Him.
You squint and see double because you've strayed
and disbelieved.'

The dust of saying 'How?' and 'Why?' brought
down a barrier
Between the Envious One's eyes and the
star of good fortune.

The star says, 'Go away; may you become
even more veiled:
Bereft of my company, and also of [the Divine] Presence.'

Many questions and answers are contained
within that veil.
Have you not seen the way Abraham was
veiled from Nimrod?

Oh God, what a strong barrier is envy between friends!
Yesterday they were a single soul; today they're
wild wolves!

What a barrier! Before that barrier came to exist,
Iblīs, prostrating, would traverse the roof of
skies and Earth.

With joy, enthusiasm, tenderness and neediness,
And communing [with God] in many ways,
affection grew.

The veil of envy has turned him into an ass on ice;
The filth of all that [evil] has tainted his wings
and feathers.

God drove him from the heavens' mosque:
'Begone, you are unclean!'
He did not heed the message, but 'refined'
his uncleanness.

'Why should I leave? What proof? What have
I done? What is the cause?
Let us discuss [the matter], Unique and
Most Loving Lord.

If there is evil, it is You who did it: every act is Yours:
The deviance of idolatry, and of Christians and Jews.

You made me go astray – and it was You who
wished it so.
I'll make it so that You can't find one man
worthy of praise.'
(D II pp. 211–212; from ghazal 914)

*L*earned, cunning and relentless, our *'manifest foe'*
(Qur'an 36: 60, etc.) does his best to make himself
inconspicuous in order to carry out his work with
maximum effectiveness. In the present day he has
achieved such success that, even among those who do
believe in God, there apppear to be many who bearly
recognize Satan's existence, much less the extent of
his influence. It is vital to understand that he has been
around for long enough to know all about humanity's
weak spots; and that he particularly relishes the
challenge of luring people who are virtuous and/
or are interested in religion, who consequently face
especial dangers against which they may mistakenly
feel secure. Also easy targets are loners and/or people
full of sullen resentment and frustration, such as the

quiet, reclusive type who ('inexplicably') takes a gun and commits mass murder.

Satan even argues with God Himself (see above) and has a line of argument ready for every human type. For the young and angry, for example: 'Look, the Muslims everywhere are suffering. If you're a real believer and not a hypocrite, prove it. Go and kill some ordinary non-Muslims – that's what they all deserve, anyway – and then you'll go straight to Paradise with the martyrs.' For the well-intentioned person trying to improve their spiritual life: 'You are just a hypocrite, trying to be better than others so you can show off your piety!' Or, 'Can't you see what a mess you are? You'll never succeed, so why bother trying?' Or, in an attempt to make them fail by setting their sights too high, 'Is that the best you can do? That's pathetic!' And so on, depending on where our vulnerabilities lie. God be our refuge from Satan and his wiles!

GUIDES & HELPERS:
PROPHETS, SHAYKHS,
AND SAINTS

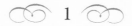

1

The Light of God Protects and Helps

Why should that Majestic Light not stand guard,
  If it can produce thousands of shining suns?

Keep travelling in safety by His Light,
  Amid those dragons and those scorpions.

That Pure Light goes ahead, leading the way,
  And tearing to shreds every highwayman.
                                    (M IV, 608–610)

The Blessed Prophet supplicated to God to grant him light in his heart, tongue, hearing and sight, before and behind him, to his right and to his left, and above and below him (Bukhārī, *Ṣaḥīḥ*). Such a guiding and helping light does not come the way of all human beings as of right, without effort on their part. We are in this world to prove ourselves of some worth to our Creator by struggling against the forces of darkness ('dragons and scorpions') and the 'highwayman' of the *nafs* (the ego), which tries to deter or hijack our efforts to live righteously. The Devil is routed and thwarted by light, which he detests. The light of faith is increased by goodly actions; and the best of actions, according to hadiths (*Sunan*s of al-Tirmidhī and Ibn Māja), is the remembrance of God (*Dhikr Allāh*). The Pure, and Majestic Light by which we are enabled to travel safety is the light of true knowledge, more glorious than a thousand suns; every form and mode of true religious knowledge is like a radiant sun that warms, guides, and enlightens us.

Dhikr Allāh, Remembrance of God

ذكر حقّ پاكست. چون پاكى رسيد

رخت بر بندد، بـرون آيـد پليـد.

مـى گـريزد ضـدّها از ضـدّها؛

شـب گريزد چون بر افروزد ضيا.

چـون در آيـد نـامِ پاك انـدر دهان

نـى پـليـدى مـانَد و نـى انـدُهـان.

Remembrance of God is something pure:
when purity comes, impurity leaves.

Opposites flee from their opposites:
Night runs away when dawn's light breaks.

When the Pure Name enters the mouth
No impurity or woes remain.

(M III, 186–188)

*T*he devotional practices and spiritual exercises known collectively as *Dhikr Allāh* (remembrance, or invocation, of God) are often associated with adherents of Sufism. *Dhikr* can take various forms, some of which are practised by Muslims of all persuasions. The Prophet Moses, upon whom be peace, was instructed by God (see Qur'an 20: 14) to establish the ritual prayer *'for My remembrance'*. But while the prayer is a powerful force protecting worshippers from bad deeds or unbecoming behaviour, *'truly the remembrance of God is greater'* (29: 45). The Qur'an also refers to itself (see e.g. 15: 9, 21: 50, 38: 87) as a *Dhikr* ('Reminder' or 'Invocation'), and also speaks of *'those whose hearts are made tranquil by* Dhikr Allāh; *is it not by* Dhikr Allāh *that hearts are made tranquil?'* (13: 28). As the author puts it: 'When the Pure Name enters the mouth / no impurity or woes remain.'

The Prophet Muhammad, peace and blessings be upon him, informed his Companions that *Dhikr Allāh* was the most meritorious of actions, and that there are angels who roam the world looking for circles of worshippers engaged in *Dhikr*, which they then outspread their wings to cover. God Himself then calls on the angels to witness that He has forgiven all those present in the circle (Bukhārī, *Ṣaḥīḥ*; Muslim, *Ṣaḥīḥ*; Aḥmad, *Musnad*). But can it really be so easy to earn such Divine Favour? The Hadiths in question are unequivocal, and our Creator has the right to decide what is most meritorious and pleasing to Him. Some Sufi authorities teach that when the Name (*al-Ism*) is pronounced and the heart is fully engaged, the Named (*al-Musammā*) becomes present, bringing '*Light upon Light*'. That 'presence' does not mean that God can ever be located, or confined within space-time; it is a matter of intensity of Divine Concern (*'ināya*) directed to those chosen to be among what the Qur'an (56: 11, 83: 21, 83: 28) calls *al-Muqarrabūn*, '*those brought nigh* [*to Him*].'

3

Physicians of the Spirit

We are spiritual physicians, disciples of God:
The Red Sea beheld us, *and parted asunder.*

Those natural physicians are different, for they
Examine the heart by measuring a pulse.

We see into hearts with ease, and directly;
Through clairvoyance we see from a place high above.

Those other physicians, with their food and fruit –
All they can do is strengthen the animal soul.

We're physicians who can treat actions and words:
Divine Majesty's ray of light is our inspirer.

To other physicians, urine samples are evidence;
This evidence of ours is the Almighty's inspiration.

We wish for no payment from anybody:
Our recompense comes from a sanctified Place.

Listen: come here for cures for 'incurable' disease!
One and all, we're a cure for the spiritually sick.
(M III, 2700–2709)

*I*t is a blessing, and often vital, to be treated for phys-
ical ailments. Treatment for spiritual ailments may
seem a less pressing need, but in reality is far more
important. The poet contrasts the purposes and pro-
cedures of the 'doctors' (a title that properly means
'teacher' or 'learned person' but was adopted by the
medical profession during the nineteenth century)
of the body with those of the doctors of the heart.
The latter, the Prophets and the Shaykhs of the Path,
make their diagnoses by seeing into people's hearts
through divine guidance and inspiration, piercing
through the normal barriers to perception as Moses
parted the Red Sea.

Even seemingly incurable diseases of the soul may
be remedied by following the spiritual physicians'
'prescriptions', provided that the patient truly wishes
to be cured. Neither the Emissaries of God nor the
masters of the Way seek any form of payment for
their work, which is all carried out purely for the
good pleasure of God; several Qur'anic verses (e.g.
26: 109, 127, 145, 164, and 180) recount how one
Prophet or another told the community to which he
was sent, *'I ask of you no recompense; my recom-
pense is from God alone.'* There is a price to be paid
to God Himself for the remedy, though it is trifling
compared with the benefits on offer: acceptance that
the ailment exists, sincere repentance, and firm resolve
to change for good.

4

The Unlettered Prophet

'Anyone who's alive can know that which has been.
He who knows what shall be – he is something else!'
(Sanā'ī, *Ḥadīqat al-ḥaqīqa*)

Muhammad, you were illiterate and you were an
orphan. You had no father or mother to take you to
school or teach you writing and other skills. From
where did you learn all these thousands of branches of
knowledge and learning? Yet you narrated from His
volume, step by step, all that has come into the world
from the very beginning of existence onwards. You told
of the [eternal] happiness or misery that He bestows.
You described the Garden of Paradise, tree by tree; the
earrings of the houris; every corner and pit of Hell. You
taught about the end of the world and the everlasting
life hereafter. From where did you learn all this?
Which school did you go to?

He replied: 'Since I was an orphan and had nobody,
that One who befriends those who have nobody was
my Teacher. He taught me: "*The All-Compassionate
taught the Qur'an*" (Qur'an 55: 1). Had I had to learn
it from mortals, I could not have done so in a hundred
years – or in a thousand. And even if I had, that

would have been acquired, imitative knowledge, the
keys of which are not in the hand of the knower, so
that it is locked up rather than inculcated ... That
is the outer form, not the reality or the spirit of
true knowledge.'

(MS 7, 119–120)

One of the titles given to the Prophet Muhammad
(peace and blessings be upon him) in the Qur'an is
'the Unlettered Prophet' (*al-Nabī al-Ummī*). Among
the special distinctions of the Seal of the Prophets is
that he was granted certain forms of knowledge that
no other human being has ever possessed. To cite but
one example: a Hadith narrated from Ḥudhayfa, an
eminent Companion, recounts that 'The Emissary of
God delivered before us an address ... from which he
did not omit anything that would happen until the
Last Hour,' including three hundred disasters and
the names of those who would instigate them (Abū
Dāwūd, *Sunan*; Muslim, *Ṣaḥīḥ*; Bukhārī, *Ṣaḥīḥ*).

'Anyone who's alive can know that which
has been.
He who knows what shall be – he is something
else!'

None of this knowledge came from study of
previous Scriptures, although the Prophet did relate
to his Companions something of the teachings of
other Revealed Books. Even if he had spent his entire

lifetime studying, he still could not have acquired all the knowledge that he taught so eloquently and compellingly. How can all this be explained except as one of the Prophet's God-given miracles?

No Spiritual Travel without a True Shaykh

Go, seek refuge in the shadow of a wise man,
To escape the foe who plots against you in secret.

This is the best of all acts of worship for you:
You will outstrip all those who have forged ahead.

Once you've chosen a Shaykh, don't be feeble-hearted;
Don't be weak and crumbly like water and earth.

And if every blow gets you full of anger,
Unless burnished how can you become a mirror?

Once the Shaykh has accepted you, surrender yourself.
Like Moses, submit to Khiḍr's command.

Bear with Khiḍr's actions without hypocrisy,
Or Khiḍr will say, 'Go! This is where we part.'

If he breaks a boat, still do not breathe a word.
If he kills a child, don't make the least thing of it.

Since God has called the Shaykh's hand His own,
By saying 'Allah's Hand is over their hands,'

The Hand of God moves him, brings him to life;
Not only brings life, but makes him everlasting.

If some rare exception travelled this Way alone,
He too did so thanks to the help of the Shaykhs.

The Shaykh's hand is not withheld from the absent:
His hand is none other than God's Handhold.

If such robes of honour are given to the absent,
Those present are better than them, without doubt.

Since they provide food to those who are absent,
What treats they must place before one who is there!

How is he who gets ready to serve in their presence,
Compared to one who is left outside the door?
(M I, 2970–2980)

*F*or those who have grasped the uncomfortable
truth that mankind faces in Satan an enemy who is
unrelenting but is hidden from us, it is not hard to see
the importance of finding a reliable guide and ally in
the struggle against the Adversary. Mawlānā Rūmī
urges us to do so, and then to be unwavering in our
resolve to follow their guidance and instructions,
regardless of whether we understand the reasons. It
is important to realize the true stature of the Shaykh

and his function, and not to be distracted by his basic human qualities:

> Make your mind the companion of a perfect
> Shaykh's mind
> So that your intellect may retreat from its
> bad habits.
>
> > (*Mathnawī* V, 738)

Again:

> Be sure to fly only with the wings of
> the Shaykh,
> So you may see the help that his armies
> will bring.
>
> Sometimes his mildness's wave becomes
> your wing;
> Sometimes his rigour's fire will drive
> you forwards.
>
> Don't think that his rigour and mildness
> are opposites:
> See how these two become as one in
> their effects.
>
> > (*Mathnawī*, IV, 544–546)

The polishing of the heart cannot be accomplished without friction. Sometimes, like the Prophet Moses with al-Khiḍr (Qur'an, *Sūrah al-Kahf*, 18) we cannot discern the wisdom behind their words and actions; but they must be accepted without question. According to the author, obedience to the Prophets, and to those Shaykhs who have Divine authorization through their links to the Final Messenger (*ṣallā Allāh ʿalayh wa sallam*) is like obedience to God Himself: '*Those who pledge allegiance to you pledge allegiance to none other than God; God's Hand is above their hands. So whoever reneges does so only to their own detriment; and whoever is true to the pledge he made to God shall have an immense reward*' (Qur'an 48: 10).

The poet does not, of course, mean that the Shaykhs are immortal, but that the effects of their presence in the world endure even after they pass on to the *Barzakh*, the Interworld between this life and the Next. 'The Shaykh's hand is not withheld from the absent.' Such is the power of his influence, thanks to Divine Providence, that even those who have never seen or met him may hope to benefit from his help and blessing. The advantages they gain cannot, however, compare with those gained from being in the Shaykh's presence and being 'present' with him in one's heart.

6

The Saint's
Self-Knowledge

The human being is the astrolabe of God, but it takes
an astronomer to know about astrolabes. Supposing
a leek-seller or a greengrocer had an astrolabe, what
use would it be to them? How could they tell from
that astrolabe the states of the heavenly spheres, the
revolution of the constellations, their influences and
turning about, and so on? For an astronomer, however,
the astrolabe is useful, for according to a wise saying
often quoted by Sufi masters, *'He who knows himself
knows his Lord.'* Just as this copper astrolabe is a
mirror of the heavens, so the human being is an
astrolabe of God: *'And We have ennobled the
Children of Adam'* (Qur'an 17: 70).

When God Most High enables a person to know, be
acquainted with, and be aware of themselves, thanks to
the astrolabe of their own being, they may witness God's
self-manifestation and His indescribable Beauty from
moment to moment, from glimpse to glimpse, and
that Beauty is never absent from that mirror. God,
Mighty and Glorious is He, has servants who clothe
themselves in wisdom, gnosis, and miracles, even though
other people lack the insight to see [such people].

They conceal themselves out of extreme jealous self-protectiveness (*ghayrat*). As al-Mutanabbī puts it:

> They wore fine dresses, not to adorn themselves
> But to keep their beauty safely hidden in them.
> (FMF no. 2, 10; DOR 22; SOTU 11)

*A*n astrolabe is an instrument designed to help those travelling by sea or on land to navigate by reference to the stars. In describing the human being as an astrolabe, Mawlānā Rūmī has in mind that such a device is based on a representation of the heavens engraved upon metal, while a human is a microcosm, a concise reflection or summation of the cosmos. In its positive aspect, the human body, with its vertical posture, complex integration, and harmonious composition, possesses the nobility ascribed to humankind by our Creator in the Qur'anic verse quoted.

The same applies with greater force to the human soul. The human heart is like a mirror, which when fully purified reflects continually the magnificence and beauty of the Divine Attributes. *'He who knows himself knows his Lord.'* So even in this worldly life, unknown to others, those 'servants who clothe themselves in wisdom, gnosis, and miracles' behold their Lord in His glory and perfection. Most conceal their state, to avoid jealousy and misunderstanding – and to avoid being praised; for any praiseworthy quality a human being can acquire is due wholly to Divine generosity.

WINGS TO FLY WITH:
FEAR, HOPE, AND
LOVE

'Read your Record While Still in this World'

آن یـکی را در قیامــت زْ انتبـاه
در کف آید نامـهٔ عصـیانْ سیاه.
سرْسـیاه چون نامـه هـای تعزیـه
پُر معـاصی متنِ نامه و حـاشیه.
جمله فسق و معصیت بُد یکسَری
هـمچو دار الـحرب پُر از کافـری.
آنچنـان نامـهٔ پـلیدِ پرْ وبـال
در یمـین نـاید، در آید در شمـال.
خـود هـمینجا نامـهٔ خودرا ببین:
دستِ چپ را شاید آن یا در یمین؟

موزهٔ چپ، کفشِ چپ هم در دکان

آنِ چپ دانـش پیـش از امتحـان.

چون نباشی راست می دان که چپی

هـست پیـدا نعرهٔ شیـر و کپی.

آنک گل را شـاهد و خوش بو کنـد

هـر چپی را راست، فضل او کنـد.

هـر شمـالی را یمینـی او دهــد؛

بحـر را مـاءٌ مَعینـی او دهــد.

Somebody, awaking to the Resurrection,
Is handed the scroll of his sins. It is dark!

Like a letter of mourning it's headed in black;
The scroll's centre and margins are filled up with sins –

All corruption and sin from one to the other;
Filled with unbelief, like the Domain of War.

A scroll so foul and noxious simply will not go
Into any right hand, but head for the left.

Here below, too, consider the scroll of your deeds:
Will it be fit for the left hand, or the right?

You can tell in the shop, before trying them on,
Which one of a pair is the left boot or shoe.

If you are not 'right', know that you must be 'left';
The cries of an ape and a lion are distinct.

Yet the grace of the One who makes flowers beautiful
And fragrant can turn all that's 'left' into 'right'.

He can turn 'Companions of the Left' to the Right,
And turn salty sea into *clear spring water*
(Qur'an 67: 30)

So if you are 'left', get 'right' with [God's] Majesty,
That you may see His kindnesses prevail for you.
(M V, 2151–2160)

On the Day of Judgement everyone who ever lived will be given a complete record of their deeds and words. The Qur'an describes tersely but graphically the momentous and terrifying nature of this experience and warns us to be mindful of it. Equally vivid is the picture Rūmī conjures up: the misdeeds of a lifetime recorded in their entirety, complete in every detail, taking visible and tangible shape in a document one is compelled to take and read. '*Read your Record: today you are sufficient as reckoner against yourself*' (Qur'an 17: 14).

Next, the poet counsels us to call ourselves to account before we are called to account. How do we know where we stand right now? By examining our consciences we should be able to tell, just as we can tell a left shoe from a right one. Rather than being complacent and giving ourselves the benefit of the doubt, we must make every effort to rectify matters in this world before it is too late. If on our present record we seem destined to be numbered among those referred to in the Qur'an (56: 41) as *'the Companions of the Left'*, those doomed to Hell-Fire, we must repent and help God the Most Merciful to turn us into *'Companions of the Right'* (Qur'an 56: 27, 38, 90, 91).

2

Self-Reproach: The World is a Mirror

Someone said, 'We are at fault.' [The Master] said: 'The fact that someone thinks this and reproaches himself, saying, "Alas, what am I about? Why do I act like this?" is a proof of God's love and favour: "*And love lasts as long as the reproach lasts.*" For one rebukes those one loves, not strangers. Now, there are different kinds of reproach. To suffer pain while being aware of it is proof of Divine love and favour. On the other hand, when a kind of pain is inflicted but the one rebuked experiences no pain, there is no proof of love (as when one beats a carpet to get the dust out), and that is not called a rebuke by the intelligent. If, on the other hand, one rebukes a child or [other] beloved, proof of love does arise in such a case. So as long as you experience pain and regret within yourself, it is proof of God's love and favour.

When you see a fault in your brother the fault really lies in you, but you see it reflected in him. Likewise, the world is a mirror in which you see your own image. "*The believer is a mirror to the believer.*" Rid yourself of your own defect, for what distresses you in another is actually something in you. An elephant was led to

a spring to drink water. He saw himself [reflected]
in the water and he recoiled, imagining that he was
recoiling from another [elephant], and unaware
that it was himself he was recoiling from.

When all the bad traits of character are there inside
you – injustice, malice, envy, greed, pitilessness, and
arrogance – you are not distressed by them. Yet when you
see them in someone else you recoil, disgusted. No one is
repelled by a scab or abscess of his own. Anyone can put
his own wounded finger into a stew and then lick that
finger without feeling at all squeamish. But if somebody
else has even a slight abscess or cut on their hand, you
would never be able to stomach stew which that hand
had been in. Evil traits of character are like those scabs
and abscesses: no one is offended by their own, but they
are upset and horrified if they see even a little in someone
else. Just as you shy away from them, you must excuse
[another] for shying away when disgusted at you. Your
distress is his excuse, as your distress comes from seeing
it; and he too sees the same thing. *"The believer is a
mirror to the believer."* The Prophet did not say *"The
unbeliever is a mirror to the unbeliever"* – not that an
unbeliever cannot [in principle] be a mirror, but because
he is unaware of the mirror of his own [soul].'
(FMF no. 6, 23; DOR 35–36; SOTU 24–25)

*T*he dictum 'The believer is a mirror to his believing
brother' is part of a Hadith (Bukhārī, *al-Adab al-
mufrad*). One of life's harder lessons to learn is to
accept when one is at fault, and not to attribute the
fault to others in an attempt to escape responsibility

and facing up to one's own defects. Rūmī shows that to be reminded of one's faults is really a blessing, whereas looking at others' faults, let alone speaking of them, entails bad consequences. Indeed, to incur a rebuke from someone, and to feel pained at realizing one's own faults, are signs of Divine favour for those with insight into the human situation. Such individuals will not rush to defend themselves, or to counterattack, when criticized. Even if the criticism is not wholly justified, the reminder of one's imperfection is still valuable.

Although one may not agree that no-one is repelled by their own scabs and abscesses – or at least the physical ones – Mawlānā points out an important psychological fact: the faults to which one is most sensitive when observed in others tend to be the kind that we ourselves possess. 'Rid yourself of your own defect, for what distresses you in another is really something in you.' Here is a key to understanding what it is that needs correcting most in ourselves. We may readily detect faults, and acknowledge their ugly, repulsive character, when they are manifested in others – but with our own faults it may be another story. That has to change, and moreover 'Just as you shy away from them, you must excuse [another] for shying away when disgusted at you.'

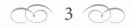

3

Do not Give Up Hope

امید از حق نباید بریدن. امید سر راه ایمنی است.
اگر در راه نمیرود، باری سر
راه را نگاه دار. مگو که «کژی هـا کردم»؛ تو راسـتی
را پیـش گیر، هیـچ کژی
نمـاند. راست همچو عصای موسی است؛ این کژی
ها همچون سـاحرها است.
چون راست بیاید، همـه را بخـورَد. اگر بدی کرده ای،
با خود کرده ای. جفای تو
به وی کجا رسد؟
[شعر]: مرغی که بر آن کوه نشست و بر خاست
بنگر که در آن کوه چه افزود و چه کاست؟

چون راست شوی آن همه نمِاند. امید را زنهار مَبرُ.

One must not give up hoping in God, for hope is the first
step on the way to salvation. Even if you do not travel
the road, at least keep the way open. Do not say: 'I have
done crooked things.' Take the straight way, and there
will be no crookedness. Straightness is the attribute of
the staff of Moses; the crooks are in the staffs of the
sorcerers. When straightness (or truth: *rāstī*) comes, it
devours them all. If you have done evil, you have
done it [only] to yourself. How could any evil
that you may have committed affect Him?

A bird perched on that mountain, then flew off.
Look: what did that mountain gain or lose?

Once you get yourself straight, none of that is left
[to harm you]. Make sure you never ever give up hope!
(FMF no. 2, 9; DOR 21; SOTU 9–10)

*I*t is interesting that in this heartening passage
Mawlānā Rūmī makes no explicit reference to Divine
Compassion and Forgiveness; instead, the emphasis is
on the fact that human sins cannot harm the Creator
in the slightest. But although we may be weak and
discouraged by the apparent difficulty of taking the
initiative by following the spiritual Way to remedy
them, we must 'at least keep the way open' – not
allowing negative thoughts to dim our hopes in God
or in our ability to mend our ways. Likewise, there
is no explicit mention of the key concept of *tawbah*,
or repentance. Instead, we are simply urged to 'take

the straight way' and not to tell ourselves that we have gone astray.

This is not a facile piece of 'feel good' philosophy of the kind often misattributed to this author, who would actually be the last person to suggest that repentance and self-reform are not essential. What he means is that we must never lose hope and become convinced that we are irremediably astray and/or that we cannot be forgiven. The imperative to repent sincerely, make amends to those one has wronged, and start anew is, however, implicit in the exhortation to 'get yourself straight' and in line with the Truth. We must have sincere resolve and confidence in our Creator that through both easy and hard times He always cares for us, providing aid and guidance to help us gain the success He wants for us. Provided we maintain this trust and resolve, there is every reason to be hopeful.

Elsewhere (*Dīwān*, vol. 2, p. 129, ghazal 765) Mawlānā tells us never to give up, even if we fear that God has rejected us. If He puts those who seek Him through trials, it is purely for our ultimate good:

Hey! If the Beloved sends you away,
do not give up hope.
If He dismisses you today, won't He
call you back tomorrow?

Should He close the door on you don't
go away, but stay and wait there;
And then, if you have been patient, He'll
seat you in a place of honour.

And if He should bar against you every
way and every passage,
He will then show you a way through –
one that nobody else knows of.

4

A Taste for Spiritual Company

A villager came to town and stayed as the guest of a town-dweller, who brought him some halva to eat. He ate it with relish and then he said: 'Townsman, I had learned to eat carrots, night and day. Now that I've tasted halva, I can't imagine enjoying the taste of carrots any more. But I won't be able to find halva all the time; and what I used to have doesn't appeal to me. What am I to do?' Once a rustic has tasted halva he is drawn to the town! The townsman has captured his heart, and he cannot help but follow in the footsteps of his heart.

There are some people who speak a greeting and the smell of smoke issues from their greeting. There are some who speak a greeting and the smell of musk issues from their greeting. Such an odour can only be detected by those with sensitive noses. One must put his friend to the test, to avoid having cause to regret in the end. That is the way ordained by God: '*Begin with yourself.*' If your self claims to be a [sincere] servant, do not accept that from it without putting it to the test.
(FMF no. 50, 188; DOR 196–197; SOTU 197)

stensibly this is a story about the contrast between the urban and rural ways of life. The last two centuries have seen a mass movement of population from the countryside to towns and cities. In recent times this, coupled with technological developments, has led to the appearance of megacities of a size and density that people of early times would have found inconceivable – and probably quite terrifying. Though town life in mediaeval times was far simpler, it still may have been very difficult for a simple rustic to adapt to. This vignette about town and country life, however, centres on the impact of an experience that causes the orientation of one's life to change so drastically that one can no longer imagine going back to where one was before, so distasteful has it come to seem.

But this tale may also be interpreted as having a more specific meaning, if we take the halva as symbolizing not a gourmet treat but a spiritual experience, often referred to in the literature of Sufism as 'tasting' (*dhawq*). One of the forms this 'tasting' may take is that while in the company of enlightened souls we may be blessed to sense, and perhaps even to share – if only in an attenuated measure – something of their elevated state. More generally, and in the longer term, the company of a Sufi master and disciples may lead a former outsider to the point where the spiritual Path has an irresistible attraction, so that they cannot think of returning to their former way of life.

In his next discourse (*Fīh mā fīh*, pp. 191–192; cf. *Discourses*, p. 201 and *Signs*, pp. 201–202), Mawlānā Jalāl al-Dīn observes that even if you continue to associate with people whose company is no longer congenial, it is never the same as before:

> Once someone has become attached to us and become drunk on this wine, wherever he goes, whomever he sits with, and whatever people he may speak with, he is in reality sitting with us. He mixes with that other kind because the company of those of another kind is a mirror that reflects the delight of being with the beloved. Mixing with those of another kind brings about love and intimate friendship with one's own kind. 'Things are made clear by their opposites.'

5

Guidance by Light and Revelation

It is said that after the Prophet and the Prophets
of old, nobody else will receive Prophetic revelation.
Why? Revelation does in fact come to people, but
it is not called Prophetic Revelation: it is what the
Prophet meant when he said, *'The believer sees by the
Light of God.'* When one sees by God's Light, one
can see everything: the beginning, the end, the visible,
the invisible. How could anything keep out the Light of
God? If it can be kept out, it is not the Light of
God. The inner meaning of Revelation is there,
even if it is not known by that name.
(FMF no. 31, 128–129; DOR 139; SOTU 135–136)

*M*awlānā Jalāl al-Dīn contends that although there
can be no Prophet after Muhammad, the Seal of the
Prophets, there is a form or mode of revelation that
still comes to certain individuals. The Qur'an tells

of Divine inspiration or revelation (*waḥy*) coming to people other than Prophets, such as the mother of Moses. Moreover, in Qur'an 16: 68–69, bees are spoken of as recipients of *waḥy*: '*And your Lord inspired* (awḥā ilā) *the bees: "Build homes in the hills and in the trees and in woven* [*hives*]. *Then feed upon all kinds of fruits, travelling the paths your Lord has paved for you ..."*' According to a Tradition of the Prophet, peace and blessings be upon him, the only thing akin to Prophethood after his own time is a dream that tells or reflects the truth.

That God's Light may guide even ordinary believers is evident from a *ṣaḥīḥ* (super-authenticated) hadith (Tirmidhī, *Sunan*): 'Be wary of the insight of the believer, for he sees by the Light of Allah.' All this shows that the light which our senses can perceive is only one form, or modality, of what light is. The fact that the Blessed Prophet used to pray for light all around him and in his hearing and sight implies that light is linked not only to perception but to understanding. Whatever share of light a mortal human may possess can only come from one source: al-Nūr (Light), one of the Names of God.

As we read elsewhere in this *Treasury*, 'things are made known by their opposites.' Now, imagine the plight of those deprived of all inward light (the spiritually, not the physically blind); '*and whoever God makes no light for has no light*' (Qur'an 24: 40). Beyond that level, as the Qur'an (24: 35) tells us, '*God is the Light of the Heavens and the Earth*':

that is, the Light of every order of created existence from the highest to the lowest. So 'When one sees by God's Light, one can see everything: the beginning, the end, the visible, the invisible. How could anything keep out the Light of God?'

6

Time for Prayer

The prayer is five times daily, but the guideline for lovers
Is the verse that says *'they who are constantly in prayer.'*

The wine-headache in those heads cannot be relieved
By five times, or even by five hundred thousand.

'Visit once a week' is not the ration for lovers;
The souls of true lovers have a craving for drink.

'Visit once a week' is not the ration for those fishes,
For they feel no spiritual joy without the Sea.

Such is the fishes' yearning that this Sea's water,
So vast, is just one gulp, too little to sate them.
(M VI, 2669–2673)

*T*he Arabic term generally translated as 'prayer' or
'ritual prayer' is *ṣalāt*. The verb root *ṣ-l-w* is said to
be linked with another, *w-ṣ-l*, which has the meaning
of 'connecting' or 'reaching'. From that perspective it
may be said that the basic idea behind the obligation

to perform *ṣalāt* at least five times in every twenty-four hour period is to do with regularity in 'contacting headquarters', so to speak – the headquarters of the Lord of All Existence – to express one's servanthood and to seek His help and blessing. Not that God has any need to hear from us; it is for our benefit. To most people today the idea of worshipping in such a visible, demonstrative manner marks out Muslims as strangers, and indeed the Blessed Prophet foretold that the time would come when Islam would again become a stranger in the world, as it was when he first proclaimed its message. At the same time, the sight of Muslims praying may evoke more positive feelings in those with some receptivity to the notion of the sacred.

For those in love with God, offering *ṣalāt* is less a matter of fulfilling an obligation than of keeping an appointed tryst. The phrase 'Visit once a week' is quoted from a (weak) Hadith according to which the Prophet, peace and blessings be upon him, advised believers to maintain their mutual affection by restricting themselves (in normal circumstances) to visiting each other 'now and then' to avoid the risk of tedium. Devotees of Divine Love, however, are not content with even five 'visits' daily. They need to be immersed always in consciousness of the Divine, as a fish needs to be in the sea; and to revel not only in its revivifying liquidity and freshness but also in its boundlessness.

A Qur'anic verse (70: 23) is cited here which is normally understood as praising, and deeming successful, those true believers who are '*constant in their prayers*'; the poet interprets it instead as referring to those who are '*constantly at their prayers.*' In one of his discourses, too, he speaks of the ritual prayer as a state of being, something still greater than the action of praying. Alluding to *ṣalāt* as a 'visit' underlines that it is essentially a means of contact and communication between human servant and Divine Master. According to the Qur'an (20: 14) the Prophet Moses was ordered to '*... worship Me and establish the* ṣalāt *for My remembrance*'; and (29: 45) '*the ritual prayer deters from indecency and wrongdoing, but truly the remembrance of God is greater.*' Underlying every ritual (a word that properly signifies not a meaningless routine but a means of contact with the Divine), and every act of worship, is a mystery, an inner reality that the mind cannot wholly grasp.

7

The Voice of Longing: A Letter in Verse

Finest one in the world, peace be upon you.
My sickness and my health are both in your hands.

Though I cannot come to your presence in person,
My spirit and my heart are present with you.

If speech cannot reach you without spoken words,
Why is the world filled with the call *'Here for you!'*?

Ill fortune is telling you: *'Transform me, please!'*
Good fortune tells you: *'O how lucky you are!'*

Many an 'Alas!' said to you, for your sake;
'Alas! Rescue me!' said to you, thanks to you.

Tell me, what is the cure for your servant's sorrow?
The kiss of light I had from those lips of yours.

Shams-i Dīn, may you savour life with the Beloved,
Because He is manifested *in your eyes.*
(Aflākī, *Manāqib al-ʿārifīn*, ed. T. Yazıcı, vol. 2, p. 702)

*F*ollowing the disappearance of Shams-i Tabrīzī, Jalāl al-Dīn Rūmī sent his son Sulṭān Walad to go and search for him. Walad was also entrusted with missives, in the form of poems, to be given to Shams should he be found. The above poem is the second in the series of such letters, the texts of which are reproduced in Shams al-Dīn Aflākī's biography of Mawlānā and his circle and successors, *Manāqib al-ᶜārifīn* ('Accomplishments of the Gnostics'). It contains an eloquent plea to Shams to return to Konya with Sulṭān Walad, contending that Shams must already be aware of his plight, and of his longing to be in his company and at his service, without any words being expressed:

> 'Though I cannot come to your presence
> in person,
> *My spirit and my heart are present with you.*
>
> If speech cannot reach you without
> spoken words,
> Why is the world filled with the call
> *"Here for you!"*?'

This letter to Shams, and the first one in the series, are examples of poems that display the author's linguistic mastery in a special way. They are macaronic: in other words, they are in two different languages used alternately – in this case Persian and (where italicized above) Arabic. He also composed verses, though not entire poems, in Eastern Turkic and in Demotic Greek. Sulṭān Walad too was a prolific author, and he wrote in Turkish as well as in Persian, and in both verse and prose.

BITTER AND SWEET:
SELF-DISCIPLINE AND
SPIRITUAL PROGRESS

1

Daily Devotions and Spiritual Stations

The daily devotions (*awrād*) of seekers and wayfarers consist in occupying themselves with striving and servanthood. They divide up their time in such a way that every moment is devoted to a specific task which, like an overseer, habitually draws them to that task. When one arises in the morning, for example, that is a time most appropriate for worship because the self is more quiescent and pure. Each individual performs the type of service that is fitting for them, sizing up their noble souls: '*And truly we are the ones ranged in ranks, and we are the Glorifiers*' (Qur'an 37: 165–166). There are a hundred thousand ranks. The more pure anyone becomes, the further forward they are brought; and the less pure, the further back: '*Send them back as God has sent them back.*' This is a long story, but its lengthiness is unavoidable. Anyone who tries to shorten this story will shorten their own lifetime and their soul, *except for those whom God safeguards.*

As for the regular devotions of those who have attained the Goal, I will say as much about them as can be

understood. In the morning, sanctified spirits, pure
angels, and those creatures *'whom no one knows
but God'* (Qur'an 14: 9) and whose names He keeps
concealed from mankind out of extreme protective
jealousy, come to visit them: *'And [when] you see people
entering God's religion ...'* (Qur'an 110: 2); *'And the
angels enter upon them from every gate'* (Qur'an 13: 23).
You may be next to them, yet you cannot see. Of those
words, greetings, and laughter you hear nothing. But
what is surprising about that? A sick person close
to death may have imaginal experiences that those
next to them are unaware of and cannot hear.

'Take on the traits of God.' When that has been
achieved, *'I am his hearing and his sight'* comes to pass.
This is a most vast spiritual station. It would be an
injustice even to talk about it, since its vastness cannot
be conveyed by the letters v, a, s, and t. If even a little
of it could be grasped then no letter v, no means of
enunciating it, no hands, and no aspirations would
be left. The troops of [spiritual] lights would devastate
the city of Existence. *'Kings, when they enter a town,
ruin it ...'* (Qur'an 27: 34). A camel enters a small
house; the house is ruined, but inside the ruin are a
thousand treasures.

'Only in ruined places can treasures be found;
In a flourishing place a hound is but a hound.'

We have spoken at length of the spiritual stations
of those on the Path, but how are we to describe the
spiritual states of those who have achieved union
(*wāṣilān*), except that the latter are infinite, whereas the
former are finite? The limit of the wayfarers is union

(*wiṣāl*); but what is the limit for those in union?
A union that can never be undone by separation:
no ripe grape ever turns green again, and no mature
fruit ever becomes immature again.

'I consider it unlawful to talk with common people;
But when You are the subject my talk becomes
so lengthy!'

By God, I will not talk at length! I will cut it short.
(FMF 122–123, no. 28; DOR 132–134, SOTU 126–129)

T he word *awrād* (singular *wird*) is often used by Sufis
to mean a litany: that is, a collection of formulae
of invocation (*Dhikr Allāh*) and supplicatory
prayers (*duʿāʾ*, pl. *adʿiya*), intended for particular
times of day and/or occasions and/or for a specific
Sufi brotherhood. In the present context, however,
what are meant are devotional practices of any
kind, performed regularly at a specific time. These
form part of the regimen and training prescribed
for disciples by the Shaykh of a Sufi Order. But the
practice of having a daily routine of supererogatory
worship alongside the prayers is not confined to Sufis;
many other Muslims maintain it.

'Take on the traits of God' is frequently quoted as
a hadith, it being understood that this means to strive
to acquire the Divine Qualities to the limited extent
possible for mortal beings. 'I am his hearing and his
sight' is quoted from a well-known hadith, found in

al-Jāmiᶜ al-Ṣaḥīḥ of al-Bukhārī and the *Musnad* of Aḥmad and much loved by people of the Path:

> God Most High has said: 'Whoever shows enmity towards a *Walī* (Friend, Saint) of Mine, I declare war on him. My servant draws close to Me with nothing dearer to Me than that which I have made obligatory for him. My servant does not cease to draw closer to Me with non-obligatory works until I love him. And when I love him, I become his hearing with which he hears, his sight with which he sees, his hands with which he seizes, and his feet with which he walks. Were he to ask Me I would surely give to him; and were he to seek refuge in Me I would certainly grant him refuge.'

Contrition

O my heart, what have you thought up to
excuse these shortcomings?
On His part so much kindness; on your part
so much wrongdoing.

On His part such generosity; on yours such
wrong and inconstancy.
From His side so many blessings; from your
side so many mistakes.

On your part such envy, so many illusions,
such bad thoughts;
On His part so much attraction, so much
tasting, so many gifts.

So much tasting for what purpose? That your
sour soul may turn sweet.
So much attraction to what end? That you
may join the Friends of God.

Your badness makes you repent. You start
to cry 'Allah!'
That very moment He is drawing you to Him,
to save you.

Because of sins you grow afraid and start to
ask for remedies;
Why can't you see with you, right then, the One
who has made you fearful?

If He has closed your eyes, and you are like a
marble in His hand,
Sometimes He will roll you along, sometimes
He'll toss you in the air.

Now He implants in you the love of silver
and gold and women;
Now He puts light in your soul from the image
of the Chosen One.

Drawing you this way to the sweet, and then
that way towards the sour;
Will your vessel pass through safely, or be
broken in those whirlpools?

Make so much secret supplication, and cry out
so much in the nights,
That from the seven heavens' dome the sound
echoes back in your ears.

(D I, pp. 5–6)

These lines from one of the first poems in Rūmī's
Dīwān needs little by way of commentary. Addressing
his own heart and conscience, the poet confesses (for
the purpose of instructing the audience) that he has
failed even to aspire to match the generosity and
kindness of his Divine Master. All the difficulties (the

'tasting'), that he experiences are manifestations of God's Attribute of *Jalāl* (Majesty, or Rigour). They are not prompted by cruelty; the purpose behind the 'tasting' is that he learns to refine his soul. As for the manifestations of *Jamāl* (Beauty, or Kindness), at times these attract us to the passing riches and pleasures of this world, imperilling the fragile craft of our soul. Yet the strongest attractive force is the subtler one, the Mercy that in times when we grow fearful calls us to repent, and to implore God's help in turning us into people of 'rightness', to use an expression of Mawlānā Rūmī's (see 'Read your Record while still in this World').

3

Self-observation (Murāqaba) and Concealing Others' Faults

سِتْر کن، تا بر تو سَتّاری کنند؛
تا نبینی ایمنی، بر کس مخند.
بس درین صندوق چون تو مانده اند،
خویش را اندر بلا بنشانده اند.
آنچه بر تو خواهی، آن باشد پسند
بر دگر کس آن کن از رنج و گزند.
زانکه بر مرصاد حقّ، و اندر کمین
می دهد پاداش پیش از یَومِ دین.

آن عظیمُ الْعَرْش، عرش او مُحیط؛

تختِ دادش بر همـه جـانْ ها بسیط.

گوشهٔ عرشش به تو پیوسـته اسـت؛

هین مجنُبان جز به دین و داد، دست.

تو مُراقِب باشْ بر احوالِ خویـش.

نوش بین در داد و بعد از ظُلم، نیش

Hide others' faults, so that others may hide *your* faults.
Laugh at no one till you see that *you* are quite safe.

Many like you have been left stuck in this chest,
And have landed themselves in tribulation.

Cause only as much pain or harm to others
As you would wish for or accept for yourself.

For God is there, unseen but ever Watchful;
He may punish before the Day of Judgement.

All-Embracing is the Throne of the All-Majestic;
His Seat of Justice extends over all souls.

The corner of His Throne is in contact with you.
Don't make one move except for faith and justice.

Keep a close watch upon the states of your soul;
Find justice sweet, and poison in wrongdoing.

(M VI, 4526–4532)

*T*hese verses recall the all-important English maxim 'Do as you would be done by.' God Most High hears and sees our every word and act; as if that were not enough, He is also aware of our every thought. We are warned (Qur'an 21: 47) that on Judgement Day the Scales will be set up justly and everything must be accounted for. We are commanded (59: 18): '*Let [each] soul look to what it has sent ahead for the Morrow.*' The phrase 'The corner of His Throne is in contact with you' delivers a vivid reminder that God's Watchfulness and Justice (al-Raqīb, 'the Ever-Watchful', and al-ʿAdl, 'the Just', being two of the Divine Names) are closer at hand than one might wish to suppose.

The practice of *murāqabah*, or keeping a close watch over one's words and deeds, is fundamental to the spiritual Path. A highly developed exposition of the subject is made by Imam Ghazālī in his *Iḥyā' ʿulūm al-dīn* ('Revival of the Religious Sciences'), in which the influence of the great early Sufi al-Ḥārith al-Muḥāsibī is discernible. We are in this world on serious business and must take our transactions seriously: while worldly profit and loss last for but a few short years, the effects of profit or loss in our spiritual life are everlasting. The *nafs* or ego is like a business partner to be dealt with carefully by keeping it in its proper place, checking on it, and calling it to account. Ghazālī distinguishes six aspects of working to gain control over the *nafs*: *mushāraṭa* (laying down the rules, and penalties for disobeying them), *murāqaba* (vigilance), *muḥāsaba* (taking stock), *muʿāqaba* (punishment), *mujāhada* (spiritual striving), *muʿātaba* and *tawbīkh* (reproaching and reviling the ego). If we judge ourselves according to divinely inspired guidance, we will not be misled. To see things as they truly are is 'to find justice sweet, and poison in wrongdoing.'

4

Leave your Mind Behind

In times of pain or death you turn that way
[towards God].
How are you when your pain has gone? Ignorant!

And this comes about because, without doubt,
One who knows God is always intent on Him.

Partial Reason's sometimes on top, sometimes below;
Universal Reason's immune to disaster.

Sell Reason, and buy Bewilderment instead.
My son, go to abasement, not to Bukhara.
(M III, 1141–1143)

There can be times when one is bewildered, unable to think of a way to escape a situation, or too grief-stricken to decide what to do. Masters of the Path teach that such dilemmas are reminders and opportunities to turn to our Creator and renew our relationship with Him. In remembering our dependence on Him and experiencing His Mercy, we come to know Him better. What is the link between this theme and the point about Partial (*juz'ī*) and Universal (*kullī*) Intellect, or Reason? Rūmī means that when ordinary people, even those who are seekers of Truth, try to think their own way out of problems their perspective is normally confined to the scope of the Partial Intellect, which is all too fallible, being 'sometimes on top, sometimes below'.

By Universal Intellect (or Reason) the poet means the power of the intellect as manifested in its full power and plenitude in the Prophets and the greatest *Awliyā'* or Friends of God thanks to the light of Divine Guidance. Bukhara, for centuries one of the greatest cities of the Orient, represents the metropolis, with its abundant places of learning and material resources. 'Bewilderment' means accepting one's incapacity to find one's own way. This state of humility attracts compassion from God, '... *Who answers the hard-pressed one when he calls to Him, and removes harm?*' (Qur'an 27: 62). But the guiding light may also arrive through non-rational intuition (*Dīwān*, vol. 5, p. 132, ghazal 2335):

> 'First pass that big cup to the chattering ego,
> so its power of reason will tell no more tales.
>
> Once its talk is shut off a torrent will arrive,
> until no sign of time or place can be seen.'

Paradise is built of Goodly Intentions

هــم درخــت و مـیـوه، هــم آب زُلال
بـا بـهـشـتـی در حـدیـث و در مَقـال
زانـکـه جنّت را نـه زآلـت بسته انـد
بلكه از اعـمـال و نیّت بسته انـد.
ایـن بنـا ز آب و گِـلْ مُـرده بُـدَست
وآن بنـا از طاعـتِ زنـده شدسـت.
ایـن بـه اصلِ خویـش مـانْد: پُرخِلَل
وآن به اصلِ خود که علم است و عمل
هــم سریر و قصر و هـم تـاج و ثیـاب
بـا بهــشــتـی در سؤال و در جـواب.

فـرش، بی فرّاش پـیچـیـده شـود

خـنـه، بـی مکناس روبـیده شـود.

خـانـه دل بین زِ غـم ژولیـده شد

بی کناس از توبه ای روبیـده شد.

تـخت او، سیّار بی حـمّـال شد؛

حلقه و دَر، مُطـرب و قوّال شـد.

هسـت در دل زندگیِ دَارُ الـخُلُودْ

در زبانم چون نمی آید، چه سود؟

Trees, fruits and clear water all converse
And discourse with the dwellers in Paradise.

Heaven was not built with the use of tools,
But constructed from acts and from intentions.

That Home is not built of dead water and mud;
It is built of living acts of pious worship.

This house, like its basis, is full of faults;
That one's [strong] like its basis: knowledge and action.

Thrones, palaces, crowns and robes all converse
With the people residing in Paradise.

Carpets are rolled up without carpet-rollers;
Houses are swept clean without any brooms.

See the heart's house, with all sorrow scrubbed away;
Hearts dusted by repentance, not by sweeping!

Its sedan chairs move around, not borne by bearers;
No knockers on doors, but singers and minstrels.

Life in the Realm Eternal dwells in the heart.
I can't describe it; what's the good [in trying]?
(M IV, 474–478, 482)

A s stated in the last couplet, the beauty and delights of Paradise are miraculous beyond all imagination or description, and are everlasting. The most alluring luxuries this world can offer must surely pale in comparison; what is more, 'You can't take it with you.' How wonderfully Mawlānā Jalāl al-Dīn evokes the Afterlife of the blessed in this passage! Imagine being greeted by the glorious palaces and appurtenances of Heaven! Even in this world – 'this building ... full of defects' – some blessed souls enjoy a state of heart that is a foretaste of 'Life in the Final Abode.'

Such, then, is Paradise: infinitely precious, infinitely desirable. But it has a price: it cannot be attained without faith and striving. Mawlānā underlines that it is not only one's actions that may, God willing, help one to reach eternal happiness in the Hereafter. It is also, and above all, making good and sincere intentions. Sincerity, however, is something that can only be achieved with Divine help. Intentions being a matter of the heart, we are given a further reminder of the importance of purifying it.

6

The Alchemy of Unity

What does exalting God really signify?
Regarding your self as despicable dust.

What does learning God's Unity really mean?
Burning your self up in the presence of the One.

If you wish to shine as bright as daylight
Then burn up your self, which is dark as night.

Melt your being away in the Truly Existent;
Melt away just as copper does in elixir.

You have both hands clamped onto 'I' and 'We'.
All this spiritual ruin stems from these two.

(M I, 3008–3012)

nity (*Tawḥīd*) as a subject taught in schools and Islamic colleges is a theological principle, but the realization of *Tawḥīd* has many levels. From a Sufi perspective it is incomplete without an existential transformation taking place in the knower. There is a Qur'anic commandment (47: 19) which although phrased in the singular is understood as being addressed to every human individually: 'Know, then, that there is no god but God.' This knowledge begins with a basic understanding that there can only be one true Divinity. It ascends to progressively higher degrees of metaphysical awareness and experiential cognition: for example, that the same uniqueness is possessed by all of the Divine Attributes (*Ṣifāt*) and Actions (*Afʿāl*).

These lines from the *Mathnawī* come immediately after the story about the tattooing of the man from Qazwīn ('No Gain Without Pain'). The connection will shortly become apparent. 'What does learning God's Unity really mean?' Mawlānā asks. His immediate answer opens up a perspective of existential transformation: 'Burning your self up in the presence of the One.' This 'self' is not, of course, the self in its higher aspect: the human being as a mirror of the divine perfections. It is the *nafs*, the ego, which in its unregenerate state is a major obstacle to seeing the truth because of its individualistic nature, with 'both hands clamped onto "I" and "We".' Poets sometimes describe the *nafs* as blind, short-sighted, or squinting. Rūmī here goes further than that; after all, he is exhorting his readers to seek spiritual perfection. He calls the *nafs* 'despicable dust' and 'dark as night' and says that it needs to be burned up to give light. He then switches to another image: the soul is like copper needing to be transformed into gold by the alchemist's elixir, by which he means guidance and discipline on the spiritual Path.

The Sweetness of Self-Sacrifice

The rule of friendship is that one must sacrifice oneself for one's friend, cast oneself into the fray for the sake of one's friend. All are facing the same thing, all submerged in the same ocean. That is the effect of faith, the rule in Islam. What is a burden borne by the body, compared with a burden borne by the soul? *'No harm [for us], for unto our Lord we shall return'* (Qur'an 26: 50). When a believer sacrifices himself for God, why should he be concerned about disaster, danger, hands, or feet? As he is heading towards God, what need has he of hands or feet? [God] gave you hands and feet to use to set out from Him in this direction, but you are on your way to the Maker of all feet and hands. If you lose control and stumble, and lose your hands and feet like the sorcerers of Pharaoh, what is there to grieve over?

> One can sip poison from the hand
> Of one's silver-bosomed beloved.
> And the bitterness of her words
> Can be swallowed down like sugar.

Sweet is the Beloved – oh, how sweet!
And wherever there is sweetness,
Sorrow's bitterness can be borne.
(FMF no. 46, 177–178; DOR 185–186; SOTU 185)

'*A*ll submerged in the same ocean.' All the Children of Adam are a single entity or, as the English expression goes, we are all in the same boat. In performing acts of selflessness we show recognition of this fact. Furthermore, our own best interests lie in sacrificing (literally, 'making sacred') ourselves, following the example of the countless sacrifices made by Muhammad and the other Prophets, peace and blessings be upon them all, who were the most sorely tried of human beings.

In this passage Mawlānā Rūmī cites the Qur'anic narrative of the sorcerers of the Pharaoh of Egypt who, on seeing their magic 'snakes' devoured by the transformed staff of Moses, submitted to the One God as believers. Even though Pharaoh threatened to crucify them and cut off their arms and legs, the ex-sorcerers retorted that nothing he could do would deflect them from the guidance they had received (for this particular version of the narrative see Qur'an 26: 10–51, especially 38–51). From that determined resignation of theirs we can be certain that the sweetness of love and faith had entered their hearts. The sweetness of a beloved human makes it easy to endure any harshness from them: 'the bitterness of her words / can be swallowed down like sugar.'

What, then, of the trials sent by the Ultimate Beloved, who created everyone and everything lovable, and in whom every lovable quality exists in infinite and indescribable perfection?

The following lines from the *Mathnawī* (VI, 1966–1967 and 1979–1981), teach that 'The Madness of Love' is a blessing for those on the Path – and that while Reason looks for profit, Love is uncalculating:

How could reason travel to where no
hope lies?
It's Love that runs full-tilt in that direction!

It is Love, not the mind, that 'couldn't
care less.'
The mind seeks that which will benefit it.

…

There's nobody crazier than a lover:
His passion makes his mind blind and deaf.

What ails him is no common form of
madness;
In such cases medicine gives no guidance.

Were a physician infected with such madness,
He'd wash out his casebook with tears of
blood!'

8

The Fruits of Gratitude

To give thanks is to hunt down, or trap, one's blessings.
When you hear the voice of gratitude, you are prepared
to give more. 'When God loves a servant He tries him. If
he is patient, He prefers him; if he is grateful, He makes
him [one of the] elect.' There are those who thank God
for His cruelty and those who do so for His kindness.
Both are good. Gratitude being a remedy that changes
cruelty into kindness, the man of perfect intelligence
is one who gives thanks [even] for cruelty, whether in
company or in secret. He is one of God's elect.

...

The mention of goodness calls forth goodness,
Just as the minstrel calls forth the wine-cup.

That is why God has mentioned His Prophets and
righteous servants in the Qur'an and thanked them
for what they did for Him, the Almighty, the Much-
Forgiving. To be thankful is to suck the breast of
blessings. Even if the breast is full, milk will not flow
unless one keeps sucking. [Somebody] asked: 'What
is the cause of ingratitude, and what is it that prevents
gratitude?' The Shaykh replied, 'What prevents
gratitude is sheer greed. Anyone afflicted with it

wants more than he got, and his wanton greed
leads him to it. Since what materialized was less than
what he had set his heart on, it prevented gratitude.'
(FMF no. 48, 181; DOR 189; SOTU 188–189)

The All-Merciful Bestower normally provides for
people's needs in this world even if they fail to
give thanks, and even if they deny His existence.
Nonetheless, those who fail to show gratitude to the
One who sustains them and everything in the Universe
commit a major sin and risk losing everything. To give
due thanks involves actions as well as words: striving
to please the Giver of Sustenance. '*What will God do
with your punishment if you give thanks and have
faith?*' (Qur'an 4: 147). As Rūmī says:

> Giving thanks for blessings is sweeter than
> those blessings (*ni*ᶜ*mat*).
> Why should one who is thankful go looking
> for blessings?
> Bounties make one heedless; giving thanks
> makes one heedful.
> Hunt blessings with the net of thanking the
> Sovereign.

9

Be Tolerant of Others

O Muslim, if you seek to acquire good character –
It's nothing but putting up with the ill-mannered.

If you come across anyone who's complaining
That So-and-So has a bad nature and character,

Know that the one who complains is ill-natured –
For he is speaking ill of that bad-natured one.

The one with good character is self-effacing,
And tolerates those with bad nature and character.

Reproaches from a Shaykh, although ordained by God,
Do not stem from anger, or self-will, or caprice.
(M IV, 771–775)

*T*his passage from the *Mathnawī* echoes others in this
book: firstly 'Self-Reproach: The World is a Mirror,'
which teaches that the faults that we see and detest
in others may well be faults that we tolerate, or even
fail to notice, in ourselves; secondly, 'What You

Do is What You Get.' One of the most important character traits that the Muslim is enjoined to acquire and cultivate is that of forbearance and forgiveness towards the faults of others. Experience teaches that the faults we are most upset by when we find them in others tend to be the very faults that we are failing to discern, or to tackle, in ourselves. If only we were to grasp and face up to what is wrong with ourselves, it would be less difficult to be 'self-effacing and tolerant'. That observation does not, however, apply to the warnings, criticisms and advice addressed to us by Shaykhs and other genuine religious authorities. These come not from any fault in those people; on the contrary, they come from Divine guidance. We need to understand, heed, and appreciate them as stemming from our Creator's concern and compassion.

10

The Way of Poverty

'Whoever wishes to sit with God, Exalted is He, let him sit with the people of Sufism.' Compared with the spiritual states of dervishes, the [rational] sciences are a game, a waste of one's lifetime: '*This worldly life is but a sport.*' (Qur'an 6: 32) Now when a man has reached adulthood and is intelligent and fully developed, he no longer plays around; or, if he does, he conceals it, out of extreme embarrassment lest anyone should see him. The academic learning and chitchat and the caprices of this world are like the wind, and Man is dust. When the wind gets mixed up with dust it makes eyes sore wherever it may blow, and its presence produces nothing but confusion and aversion. Yet although Man is earth, with every word [of Truth] he hears he may weep, and his tears are like running water: '*You see their eyes overflowing with tears*' (Qur'an 5: 86). Now when water, instead of air, falls on the Earth, the opposite is bound to happen: when earth receives water, fruit, grasses, fragrant herbs, violets and roses grow.

This Way of Poverty is the way for you to achieve all that you hope for. Whatever you may have yearned for will certainly come your way by this means,

be it the defeat of armies and victory over enemies,
seizing kingdoms and subduing people, superiority
over your peers, eloquence in speaking and writing,
or anything else of that kind. Opt for the Way of
Poverty and all these things will come your way.
No one who followed this Way rather than
another has ever had cause to complain. Out of
every hundred thousand who took other ways
and struggled, only one reached his goal, and even
he did not gain a happy and peaceful heart.

Every way involves means and methods to attain the
objective, and the objective cannot be reached except
by applying them. Such a way is long, and is full of
pitfalls and obstacles which may prevent one reaching
the destination. But once you have entered the realm of
Poverty and practised it, God Most High will grant you
kingdoms and worlds such as you never imagined. You
will be embarrassed by what you had previously desired
and yearned for. You will say, 'Oh, how could I ever
have sought for something so worthless, when such a
[wonderful] thing existed?' But God Most High will say,
'Although you are now above that thing, undesirous and
disdainful of it, it did cross your mind at that time; but
you gave it up for Our sake. Our generosity is limitless,
so I will certainly provide you with that as well.' ...

So for any man who has staked his very soul upon this
Path, all his objectives – be they religious or worldly –
have become attainable. None of them has ever had
cause to complain about this Path.
(FMF no. 39, 145; DOR 154; SOTU 151)

*E*ven this short excerpt illustrates how in his discourses, as in his poems, Rūmī moves skilfully between themes while interlinking them.

He begins by underlining the importance of keeping company with people whose words and states have an uplifting effect. Next, he contrasts academic learning with mystical discourse, practice and knowledge, characterizing the former as immature frivolity of which 'grown men' should be ashamed. Next he tells us that those who weep as God's lovers do – the Qur'anic verse describes those moved by the truth and profundity of God's Revelation – have hearts in which spiritual states and gnosis grows, just as rain enriches the Earth, producing the finery of fruits and flowers.

The second paragraph outlines the nature, and the wondrous effects, of what Rūmī calls 'The Way of Poverty'. What he means here is not simply choosing to be poor and detached from the world, although clearly that is often part of this Way. The emphasis is less on *faqr* (poverty) in the literal sense and more on the state and practice of *iftiqār*, a word derived from the same Arabic root. Part of *iftiqār* is to recognize one's complete 'poverty' in relation to God, in the sense of being entirely dependent on the Divine Mercy and Generosity for anything one has or could wish to have. '*Mankind, you are the poor ones and God is the Infinitely Wealthy, the All-Praiseworthy*' (Qur'an 35: 15).

But *iftiqār* also entails acting according to that recognition. The aim is to ask that He respond to and cover our human attribute of neediness with His attribute of Wealth. Nothing that we have belongs absolutely to us; it is all an *amāna*, a trust that the Creator bestows on us and for which we shall have to answer in the Next World. Moreover, and before all that, this *iftiqār* or Way of Poverty requires that we seek that which we want or need always through God, with prayers and humility, taking the steps that are logically necessary but without ever relying on our own power or strength or assuming anything to be our natural right.

Such is the importance of this understanding that according to a Hadith, '*There is no power or strength but through* God' is one of the treasures of Paradise (Muslim, *Ṣaḥīḥ*). Moreover, the Qur'an tells us: '*And whoever is wary of God, He makes for them a way out and provides for them from where they do not expect. And whoever places their reliance upon God, He shall suffice them. Truly God shall accomplish His purpose; and God has already made a decree for all things*' (Qur'an 65: 2–3). One of the great Sufi masters, Shaykh Aḥmad Ibn ʿAṭāʾ Allāh, teaches in his *Ḥikam* or 'Wise Maxims' that 'Nothing that you seek through God is difficult, and nothing that you seek through yourself is easy (to gain).' The latter clause serves to confirm Mawlānā Jalāl al-Dīn's warning about the pitfalls and obstacles that face those who insist on relying on their own efforts and resources to achieve success, and the high risk of failure.

Lastly, as 'the poor ones' we must remember that although He promises to help those who sincerely submit to Him and support His Cause, God is not obliged to answer all our prayers exactly as and when we wish. He is the Master; we are the servants. Furthermore, the All-Wise Creator knows what is best for us. Spiritual growth may lead the seeker to give up the desire for something they once longed for, yet they may still receive it along with such things as they could never have imagined. 'So for any man who has staked his very soul upon this Path, all his objectives – be they religious or worldly – have become attainable.'

FAITH AND WISDOM:
THE *DĪN* OF ISLAM
FROM WITHIN

1

The Law, The Way, and Ultimate Truth

The Sacred Law (*Sharī'a*) is like a candle that lights
the way; without a candle to hand, the Way cannot be
travelled. When you take the Way, your travelling is
the Path (*ṭarīqa*). When you reach the Destination,
that is the Truth (*ḥaqīqa*) …

In short, the Law is like learning alchemy from a teacher
or a book; the Path is like using tinctures and rubbing
copper against the Alchemical Stone (*kīmyā'*); and the
Truth is the process of copper becoming gold.

… To put it another way, the Law is like learning the
science of medicine; the Path is following a diet, and
taking remedies, in accordance with that science; and the
Truth is gaining everlasting good health and independence
from either [medical theory or practice]. When a person
departs from this world, the Law and the Way are cut off
from him and there remains only the Truth.

… The Law is knowledge, the Way is action, and Truth
is reaching God. '*So whoever looks ahead to meeting*

*with his Lord, let him act righteously and associate no
one in the worship of his Lord.'* (Qur'an 18: 110) May
God exalt Muhammad, the best of His Creation, and his
Family and Companions, and bless them abundantly.

(M V, preface)

*H*ere the author employs a series of analogies to explain
the Sufi perspective on religion, using a distinctive
set of terms. *Sharīʿa* (normally meaning Sacred Law)
denotes learning the religion (Knowledge); *Ṭarīqa*,
applying its principles as perfectly as possible,
with the intention of drawing close to the Creator
(Action), which Sufis often term *sulūk* (wayfaring);
and *Ḥaqīqa* (Ultimate Truth or Reality), experiential
realization (which Sufis often term *taḥqīq*). What
Mawlānā here means by 'reaching God' is not, of
course, being united in the literal sense but a special
modality of knowledge; *ḥaqīqa* (or *taḥqīq*) is in fact
an advanced form of *ʿIlm* (knowledge), representing
the highest form of Certainty (*Ḥaqq al-yaqīn*). So
from the wayfarer's viewpoint the Path to God, the
Absolute Truth (*al-Ḥaqq*) is a journey from distance to
nearness, from ignorance to knowledge, from theory
to Certainty.

2

Hell Proceeds from Evil Deeds

When blows from your hand struck a
victim unjustly,
They became a tree in Hell: the *Zaqqūm*
grew from them.

When in anger you threw fire into people's hearts,
You became a source for the fires of Hell.

Since your fire was burning mankind in this world,
What was born of it was setting fire to men in Hell.

Your fire of anger attacks people here:
The fire that sprang from it assaults people there.

Your words like snakes and scorpions have become
snakes and scorpions,
And are seizing your tail, assailing you
from behind.

You kept the Friends of God waiting, and so
You will be kept waiting at the Resurrection.

Your promise 'Tomorrow' and 'The day after
that' has become
Your waiting on the Day of Gathering. Alas for you!

Your anger is the seed of Hellfire. Take heed!
Extinguish this Hell of yours, for this is a trap.
(M III, 3741–3477, 3480)

---

*I*n the Hereafter the inner reality of actions becomes manifest in visible and tangible form. Just as Paradise is made of goodly deeds, the appalling landscape of Hell is a manifestation of the inner reality of evil deeds and words. By 'keeping the Friends of Allah waiting' Mawlānā perhaps means failing to fulfil the expectations of those who were on the sinful person's side and were praying for them to reform. Elsewhere in this *Treasury*, in 'The Three Categories of Creatures', the author says about those who struggle to better themselves that the *Awliyā'* stand waiting to bring them to their own station and make them like themselves. 'Your promise …' means a promise to do good things and/or to refrain from bad ones. According to a hadith, 'One who repents is as one who has no sins left' (Ibn Mājah, Ṭabarānī, Bayhaqī, and others). For acceptance of repentance (*tawba*), however, it is essential to resolve sincerely not to repeat the offence, to ask forgiveness from anybody one has wronged, and to make amends for the harm done to them.

Night Worship

God Most High will ask mankind, assembled
for Judgement,
'Where is your gift for Me on Resurrection Day?

You have come to Us alone and bereft of provision,
Your appearance the very same *as We created you*.

Listen! What have you brought as an
offering, a gift
On homecoming, for the Day when you
rise from the dead?

Or did you not entertain any hope of returning?
Did the promise of meeting Me today seem
vain to you?'

Reader, don't you believe His promise that
you'll be His guest?
Then you'll get only dust and ashes from His
bounty's kitchen.

If you do not disbelieve it, then how can you set foot
In the Court of the Beloved with such empty hands?

Abstain for a little while from sleep and from food,
And bring along that gift for your meeting with Him.

Reduce your sleep, like *those who at night*
slumbered but little;
In the time before dawn, be of *those who*
sought forgiveness.

(M I, 3172–3179)

*E*lsewhere in this *Treasury* (see 'Bring your Heart to My Door') we read that what our Creator most *wants* from us, though He *needs* nothing, is our hearts. Here Rūmī presents a teaching related to our position as servants entirely dependent upon the Almighty and in need of His good pleasure. '*Unto Him shall be your homecoming – a true promise from Allah*' (Qur'an 10: 4). The Day shall come when humankind collectively are told: '*You have come before Us bereft, as We first created you*' (Qur'an 6: 94). If we want to have assets that will have some value before the Lord of the Universe on Judgement Day, we should make a habit of night-time worship. The author cites two acts of non-obligatory devotion praised in the Qur'an (51: 17): night prayer and supplication, and seeking forgiveness in the blessed time of *saḥar*, the last part of the night before dawn. '*They would slumber but little of the night, and before dawn they would ask forgiveness.*'

4

Zakat (Alms) and Ṣalāt (Ritual Prayer)

In zakat, overflow and increase of one's gold
is involved;
In *ṣalāt*, safety from lewdness and wrong-
doing is involved.

The zakat is the one that safeguards your purse,
The *ṣalāt* the shepherd who saves you from wolves.
(M VI, 3574–3575)

*I*n the Qur'an the ritual prayer and almsgiving are
frequently referred to together. 'Safety from lewdness
and wrongdoing' is an allusion to Qur'an 29: 45.
Ṣalāt (ritual prayer) and its purpose and benefits are
discussed elsewhere in this *Treasury*. Zakat (alms),
payable on assets above a certain amount, is a term
derived from an Arabic root meaning both 'to purify'
and 'to grow' – the effect of its payment on those who
pay, and on their wealth ('increase of one's gold').

In Islam, acts of worship (*ʿibādāt*) are also termed 'acts of obedience' (*ṭāʿāt*). Their performance can be based on compliance without any further understanding than the knowledge (essential for all believers) that they are obligatory by Sacred Law (*Sharīʿa*). This is termed *taqlīd* (imitative compliance). A higher level of knowledge involves understanding the benefits to the worshipper for performing them, apart from gaining Divine rewards for obedience. This has the merit of providing further motivation as well as raising one's understanding.

Many verse passages in the works of Rūmī impart knowledge at that level rather than exploring any higher, more mystical, aspects of the subject at hand. The author's intention was by no means confined to imparting advanced knowledge to Sufi disciples. He has messages for all Muslims, and for anyone looking to understand 'the roots of the roots of the roots of religion' – as he describes the *Mathnawī* in the preface to Book I.

5

Pilgrimage

خوش بِکَش این کاروان را تا به حجّ،

ای امیرِ «صَبْرُ مِفْتَاحُ الْفَرَجِ».

حج، زیارت کردنِ خانه بُوَد؛

حــج ربُّ الْبَیْت، مردانــه بُوَد.

Lead this caravan sweetly on the Pilgrimage,
You leader of *'Patience is the key to relief.'*

Pilgrimage is a visit to the House of God;
The manly way is Hajj to the Lord of the House.
(M IV, 14–15)

These lines are addressed to Mawlānā's close friend, disciple, and successor Ḥusām al-Dīn Chalabī, whom the author credited with providing the chief inspiration for the composition of the *Mathnawī*. The leadership of the Pilgrimage caravan he alludes to is metaphorical: he is talking about the process of composing the poem. Nonetheless, this passage has been included in this selection because of the importance of the idea of Hajj being not only a pilgrimage to the Sacred House – the Holy Kaʿba in Makkah – but also a journey to God Himself, the Lord of the Sacred House.

'Patience is the key to relief' (*al-Ṣabr miftāḥ al-faraj*), a well-known Arabic proverb, may perhaps have been a favourite saying of Ḥusām al-Dīn's. In any case it echoes the Qur'anic message (94: 5–6), '*For truly with hardship comes ease; truly with hardship comes ease*'. Alternatively, one might understand *ṣabr* here in its more active sense, as meaning 'persistence' rather than 'patience,' in that the composition of an immensely long poem requires as much of the former as of the latter.

By 'the manly way' the author means the way of accomplished travellers on the Path, regardless of gender. This usage of the word 'men' (*rijāl* in Arabic, *mardān* in Persian) occurs in the Qur'an, for instance in 24: 37, part of the passage following the famous Light Verse, with its praise for '*Men whom neither trade nor selling divert from the remembrance of God, establishing the ritual prayer* (ṣalāt), *or paying alms* (zakat).'

6

Outward Acts of Worship Attest to Inner Light

This ritual prayer, fasting, and pilgrimage
And jihad also testify to one's faith.

Giving alms and gifts, and avoiding envy
Also testify to one's inner nature.

Hospitality and meals are ways to say:
'Noble ones, we are now in accord with you.'

Gifts, presents, and offerings all testify
As if they were to say, 'I'm happy with you.'

Whoever comes forward, with money or spells,
What does it mean? 'I have a jewel within:

Abstinence's or generosity's jewel.'
These alms and this fasting attest to them both.

His fasting says, 'He abstained from lawful things:
Know that he has no link with what's unlawful.'

His almsgiving said, 'He gives of his own wealth:
So how should he ever steal from pious folk?'
(M V, 183–190)

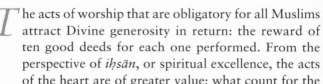

*T*he acts of worship that are obligatory for all Muslims attract Divine generosity in return: the reward of ten good deeds for each one performed. From the perspective of *iḥsān*, or spiritual excellence, the acts of the heart are of greater value: what count for the most in praying, fasting, Hajj, and fighting in defence of Islam are conviction (*iʿtiqād*) and the act of having faith – without which the intention (*niyya*) underlying their performance cannot be sincere.

These verses teach that behind every act of obligatory worship or service lies an intention, a state of heart, or a trait of character, such as generosity and abstinence from material pleasures. Each of these virtues is precious, like an inward jewel.

BEYOND DUALITY:
DILEMMAS RESOLVED

Relative Points of View

Hence there is no absolute evil in the world.
Evil is relative. Know this also to be the truth.

In the realm of Time there is no poison or sugar
That's not a foot to one, a fetter to another:

To one person a foot, to another a fetter;
Poison to one, to another sweet and healthy as candy.

A snake's venom spells life for the snake,
But to a human being it spells death.

The sea is like a garden to water-creatures;
To land creatures it is death, a painful brand.

Likewise count, O experienced man, examples
Of this relativity from one man to a thousand.

Zayd may be a devil where X is concerned,
But in the eyes of Y a beneficent sovereign.

The one and the same Zayd is a shield for Y,
While for X he is nothing but pain and loss.

(M IV, 65–73)

*A*s Mawlānā explains in another selection in this *Treasury*, there is no such thing as absolute evil; good and bad are intertwined. In the world of multiplicity and relativity, destiny often appears as a 'zero sum game': one person's good news is another person's bad news. (Candy was better 'news' in the days when it was made from unrefined organic cane sugar crystals.) The Divine Decree apportions what we perceive as favourable and unfavourable events in ways not always fathomable to humankind. It is for us to submit, and to trust in the infallible Divine Wisdom and Divine Justice.

2

Good and Evil Are Inseparable

[Someone] asked, 'Are the doer of good and evil one and the same thing?' Inasmuch as when [the doer] hesitates [between doing good or evil] they appear as contrary [choices], the answer is that they are definitely two, since one individual cannot contradict himself. From another viewpoint, however, evil and good are inextricable from one another. Evil must proceed from good, since good is abstention from evil; and abstention from evil is impossible unless evil exists. To explain [further]: if there were no motivation to evil, there would be no forsaking of good – in which case, [those] two things would not exist.

Zoroastrians say that Yazdān (i.e. Ahuramazda) is the creator of good things and Ahriman is the creator of evil and dislikeable things. To this we reply that likeable things are not separate from dislikeable ones, since the likeable cannot exist without the dislikeable. The likeable is the cessation of the dislikeable, and the cessation of the dislikeable is impossible unless

the dislikeable exists. Happiness is the cessation
of sorrow, and without sorrow its cessation cannot
exist. (The two opposites) are therefore an
indivisible unity.
(FMF no. 30, 126–127; DOR 137–138; SOTU 133–134)

*I*t seems possible that the report of the conversation
given in this passage is not completely accurate.
The Discourses as we have them today may have
been partly the product of subsequent recollection
rather than of real-time dictation. Nevertheless, the
discussion provides an important example of how
Mawlānā Rūmī dealt with theological questions.

In the first sentence, what he is trying to resolve
appears at first glance to be a 'non-problem'. It is clear
to anyone that good and evil cannot be the very same
thing. The questions to be answered, as they emerge
during the discussion without being overtly stated,
are firstly, whether both good and evil can be said to
reside in the same thing; and secondly, whether what
we call 'good' and what we call 'evil' ultimately come
both from the same source. The intended meaning of
the passage may become clearer if one rewords the
last two sentences.

First, evil cannot exist on its own. Its existence
depends upon the existence of good. Goodness is
an essential Attribute of the Lord of the Universe,
whereas evil is nothing other than the privation, or
absence, of good (just as dark is nothing other than

the absence of light, whereas the reverse is not true since Light is a Divine Name and Attribute and so its existence does not depend upon anything).

Secondly, good is the privation – or let us say, this time, 'the opposite' of evil. Therefore, if what we call 'evil' did not exist then what we call 'good' likewise could not exist. If the Zoroastrian deities of Ahuramazda and Ahriman are equal in respect of their supposed power and status, it follows that Zoroastrianism is dualism pure and simple. The response that 'good is not separable from evil' is intended here as a refutation of the Mazdaean doctrine that puts both on the same hierarchical level of existence. One additional point to note, although it is not raised in the discussion here: Rūmī's response also amounts to a refutation of the doctrine, held by both Mu'tazilite and Shia theologians, that while good is associated with the Divine Will, evil cannot be.

In another discourse (FMF 59, p. 214; SOTU p. 223), Mawlānā Rūmī argues from the standpoint that in this world, all good has some admixture of evil and vice versa:

All opposites, then, appear to be opposed to their counterparts; to the wise, however, they all perform a single function and they are not [absolute] opposites. Show me which evil there is in the world that does not contain some good, and what good there is that does not contain some evil. Suppose, for example, somebody set out to commit a murder but was side-tracked by committing fornication [instead, and so] that bloodshed did not occur.

Inasmuch as there was fornication, this is evil; but inasmuch as it prevented a murder it is good. Hence good and evil are inextricably united. On this point we disagree with the Zoroastrians, who say that there are two gods, one of whom creates good and one evil. Now, you must show us a good without evil, and then we may admit that there can be a god of good and a god of evil. That is impossible, for good is inseparable from evil; good and evil are not two things with a dividing line between them. For two Creators to exist is therefore impossible.

Mankind Has Freedom of Choice

Inward consciousness matches [outward] sense;
Dear uncle, both run within the same channel.

'Do' or 'Do not', command, prohibition,
Talk and discussion, are what concern it.

[To say] 'I will do this, or do that, tomorrow'
Proves the freedom to choose, O respected one.

When you feel repentant for an evil deed,
You've been guided thanks to your power to choose.

The Qur'an is all commands, prohibitions, threats;
Who has seen commands issued to a block of marble?

Does any man who's wise or rational do that –
Showing anger or enmity to bricks and stones,

Saying: 'I told you to act this way, or that way;
Why didn't you do so, you dead, helpless things?'

How should Reason hold sway over wood and stone?
Why should Reason take hold of a cripple with palsy

And say, 'O you slave with palsied hands
And broken legs, get a spear and go to battle'?

How [then] should the Creator, Maker of stars and sky,
Issue commands and prohibitions like such ignorant folk?

You've denied that God could possibly be powerless,
Yet implicitly called Him a stupid, ignorant fool!

...

If no one but God has the power of free will,
Why get angry with someone who does you wrong?

Why gnash your teeth at an enemy? Why
Deem the sin and offence to have come from him?

If a piece of timber breaks off from your roof,
And lands on you, causing you a severe wound,

Will you then get angry with the roof-timber,
And set about wreaking vengeance on it,

[Saying] 'Why did it hit me and fracture my hand?
It is now my foe, a mortal enemy'?

Why should you beat small children [to punish them],
While holding adults to be exempt from blame?

If a man steals your property, you will say:
'Arrest him! Jail him! Cut off his hands and feet!'

...

The anger within you is clear proof of free will;
Don't make excuses for yourself as Fatalists do.

(M V, 3022–3049)

Sufis, like mystics of other faiths, have been accused of being passive and fatalistic, prone to accept whatever happens without resistance. Here the author takes a radically different standpoint, arguing that our daily experience and discourse prove that we have been given freedom to act as we choose. But he avoids saying that this freedom is absolute, for the choices we make are the consequences of the thoughts and intentions we have, the state of our hearts, and of the way that we are; and the way that we are and the states of our hearts are not entirely of our making.

4

Divine Will is Different from Divine Contentment

God Most High wills both good and evil, but He is only pleased by good. Since He has said 'I was a Hidden Treasure and I wished to be known,' there is no doubt that God wills both positive commands and negative prohibitions. A positive command, however, only counts as such if the person being commanded is naturally averse to what he has been commanded to do. Someone who is hungry does not need to be ordered to eat sweets or sugar. If he is ordered to, that is not what one calls a command; it is in fact a favour. Again, a prohibition is not [truly] a negative command if it concerns something that a person does not want [anyway]. ... So in order for a positive or negative command to be meaningful as such, there needs to be an ego that desires that which is evil. To will that such an ego exist is to will evil; nevertheless, God is not pleased by evil.

It is comparable to a man who wants to be a teacher and who therefore wants [his] pupil to be lacking in

[some] knowledge; for if the pupil were not lacking in knowledge it would not be possible to teach them. To will something entails willing the consequences of that thing. But the teacher will not be content if the pupil continues to lack knowledge (of what they are being taught); if he were content, he would not be teaching them. In the same way, a physician who desires to practise his calling wills that people become unwell, because unless they did so it would be impossible for him to display his medical skills. But he will not be content if people remain ill [after treatment]; if he were, he would not treat them. …

Similarly, God wills that in the human soul there exist motivations to do evil. He loves a servant who is thankful, obedient and pious – but that would not be possible without the existence of such motivations in the human soul. To will something means to will all the consequences it entails; but one need not be pleased with those consequences, because one can try to eliminate them from the soul. From all this one may understand how it is that in one respect God wills evil but in another respect He does not.

(FMF, no. 47, 179; DOR 186–187; SOTU 186)

According to normative Sunni Islamic doctrine, God wills the existence of that which we call evil as well as that which we call good. All actions are created by Him in accordance with His Divine Wisdom and Justice, not with human notions of these. Muslim theologians explain this by distinguishing between on the one hand the Divine Volition (*irāda*) – that which God approves and desires (without ever being in need of anything or anyone) – and, on the other hand, the Divine Will (*mashī'a*) – that which God, in whose Hands all destiny lies, has decreed shall actually happen. Had God so wished He could have spared all humankind from any inclination to evil, but then no one could have earned any reward.

5

All Worship the Creator, Willingly or Otherwise

From cruel treatment the base become pure;
When treated kindly they themselves become cruel.

Hell-Fire's the mosque where their devotions are done;
For a wild bird, a trap is the only restraint.

For a thief and a villain the jail is a cloister,
Where he can remember God constantly.

Just as worshipping God is what man was made for,
Hell-Fire has become an oratory for rebels.

Mankind has a free hand to do anything,
But their ultimate purpose is service of God.

'I created jinn and mankind only to serve Me.'
Recite that: the world's purpose is to worship Him.
(M III, 2983–2988)

created jinn and mankind only to serve Me' (Qur'an 51: 56). In this context the interpretation of the Arabic root ⸰-b-d as 'worship' (in Persian, *ʿibādat*) is applicable, since the author has just mentioned the devotions performed by the denizens of Hell. It appears to be worship that he has in mind rather than service in general. God gives mankind a free hand to do other things besides worship. Some are clearly acts of service to the Creator; others are humanly necessary, but can be said to serve His purposes as well. For the people of the Path, every activity is a potential means of worship if accompanied by sincere intention and the remembrance of God (*dhikr Allāh*). This was beautifully expressed by a Christian poet, George Herbert (1593–1633), in 'The Elixir', which begins:

> 'Teach me, my God and King, in all
> things Thee to see
> And what I do in anything, to do it
> as for Thee.'

In the above lines from the *Mathnawī* the author opens up a new perspective on the punishment of the guilty in the Next World. Rather than being exclusively an instrument of vengeance or (for those whose punishment is of a limited duration) of atonement, Hell-Fire is also the place where the Creator is glorified – 'an oratory for rebels' – and where 'the base become pure.' So it is that in the Next World both the blessed and the damned will be engaged in worshipping their Almighty Creator.

6

A Remedy for the Restless Soul

Samāᶜ is for the soul that can find no repose.
Quick, get up! What's the point of waiting and waiting?

Don't just sit there, wrapped up in thoughts of your own.
If you're a man, go there where the Beloved is.

Do not say 'Maybe the Loved One will not want me;'
What has a thirsty person to do with such talk?

Moths do not get worried about catching fire;
For souls in love, worrying is a source of shame!

Once a warrior has heard the sound of war-drums,
At that very moment he turns into a million.

If you've heard the drum, draw your sword right away,
For your soul is the scabbard that holds Dhū l-Fiqār.

You're Ḥusayn of Karbalā'. Leave water alone:
Today's water is a shining watered-steel lance!
(D I, 203, no. 338)

*T*his is a rallying-cry to people who are hesitant to participate in *samāᶜ*, or vocal remembrance of God (*Dhikr Allāh*). Some might associate this activity with a passive and retiring attitude to life. Rūmī takes the opposite view: 'Don't just sit there, wrapped up in thoughts of your own. / If you're a man, go there where the Beloved is.' In fact, he praises *samāᶜ* as a form of spiritual combat, a dynamic remedy for the hesitant or restless soul. A healthy soul has inner resources that respond to *samāᶜ*, acquiring the strength of Dhū l-Fiqār, the deadly sword of the Imam and Caliph ᶜAlī, and the fearless resolve of his martyred son, the Imam Ḥusayn, who was murdered at Karbalā', where he and his followers suffered extreme thirst rather than capitulate to their persecutors.

7

Invocation or Contemplation?

This much we have said; now consider the rest.
If thought becomes static then go and invoke.

Remembrance brings vibrancy into one's thought;
Make remembrance a sun to thaw out what has frozen.

Attraction's the basis – but, O master and friend,
Be proactive: don't wait for that impulse to come.

Failing to do one's work is like being vain;
How can vanity stand in for total commitment?

Don't think of rejection or acceptance, my lad;
But always observe commands and prohibitions.
(M VI, 1475–1479)

The subject of this passage is one about which spiritual
authorities differ. Which is higher and more laudable:
fikr (contemplation, reflection) or *dhikr* (remembrance,

invocation)? The value of *dhikr* is discussed in (amongst others) the text '*Dhikr Allāh*, Remembrance of God'. Discursive thought, however, is ambivalent. On the negative side, the fact that the rational mind is easily misled means that thought, while indispensable in dealing with everyday matters, is not necessarily helpful in religious matters. On the other hand, since the human intellect is in principle capable of being aligned with true spiritual guidance, reflection can, if properly directed, be a means of arriving at the truth. A cogent and methodical treatment of the subject is to be found in Book 39 of al-Ghazālī's *Iḥyā' ʿulūm al-dīn*.

Rūmī elegantly resolves the dilemma by correlating *fikr* with *dhikr* and contextualizing them: 'If thought becomes static then go and invoke … Make remembrance a sun to thaw out what has frozen.'

LORD AND CHERISHER: THE RELATIONSHIP WITH GOD

1

Where is God?

Someone asked: 'Where was [God] before the Earth, Heavens, and Divine Throne existed?' We [Mawlānā Jalāl al-Dīn] replied: 'This question is invalid in itself: by definition, God has no location. Now you ask where He was before. But after all, everything around you is [also] non-spatial. Have you found where in yourself these things are that you seek? If they are non-spatial, how can you imagine a locus for thoughts and states?'

Now, the creator of a thought is more subtle than the thought itself. A builder, for instance, is more subtle than the building he has built, since he is capable of building, besides that one, a hundred other buildings and things that are not alike. Therefore, he is more subtle and precious than the building; but his subtlety cannot be perceived except through the medium of a house or some other work that comes into being in the visible world to manifest its subtle beauty.

You can see your breath in winter but not in summer. It is not that your breath ceases in summer, but since both summer and breath are subtle it does not show up, unlike in winter. Likewise, all your characteristics and substances are too subtle to be seen except through

the medium of action. God is too subtle to be visible,
so He created the Earth and Heavens so that His
omnipotent power and creativity might be seen. That
is why He says: *'Do they not look up to the sky above
them, and consider how We raised it?'* (Qur'an 50: 6).
(FMF, section 59, 212–213; DOR 219–220;
SOTU 221–222)

*H*ere Mawlānā Rūmī is called upon to answer a question
that is essentially a cosmological or metaphysical one.
When asked where God was before the Creation, the
Prophet (peace and blessings be upon him) replied that
He was in *al-ʿAmā*; this word, linked etymologically
to an Arabic word meaning 'to be blind', has
sometimes been translated as 'the Abyss'. This word
may perhaps have been chosen to convey the notion
of formless chaos – or, to express it in a more positive
way, pure Existence devoid of differentiation or
dimensionality. Rather than attempt to convey to his
audience the concept of undifferentiated pure Being,
Rūmī chooses to emphasize the point that by definition
the Divinity transcends spatiality and, for that matter,
any other attribute common (as a general rule) to
physical objects, such as visibility or touchability.

In a manner that is typical of his teaching style,
Jalāl al-Dīn elucidates his response to the question
using straightforward analogies. Firstly, if our
thoughts and our states have no location that one
can point to, how could God have such a location?
Secondly, if thoughts are too subtle to have locations

or spatial dimensions, how could the Creator of thoughts ever be characterized by them? Thirdly, take man-made objects that are visible and tangible and have a location, such as buildings: are not the builders (and/or the architects) of buildings more subtle than the edifices they create (and/or design)? On another level, just as one's breath is too subtle to be visible except in very cold weather, individual human characteristics only become visible through actions. We are in this world to manifest Divine creativity – no two human beings are identical – and because Divine Wisdom requires that we act and be judged by our actions (with consequences that are eternal).

Finally, Mawlānā addresses a question which, though not articulated in this particular discourse, logically follows the question as to where God was before the Creation: why did He, who is not in need of anything whatsoever, create anything? The Architect of the Universe, who is too subtle and sublime to be visible Himself, 'created the Earth and Heavens so that His omnipotent power and creativity might be seen.'

2

How God Provides

I know the truth about the workings of Divine
Provision, and it is not in my nature to run this way
and that in vain, or to suffer unnecessarily. Whatever
be my daily provision of money, food, clothing, or the
fire of lust, if I sit there peacefully it will come to me.
If I run around after my daily provision, the effort
will wear me out and will debase me. If I am patient
and remain where I am, it will come my way without
pain and humiliation. My daily bread looks for me,
pulls at me. When it cannot pull me, it comes, and
likewise when I cannot pull it then I go to it.

What follows from these words is that you need
to be so immersed in religious concerns that this world
comes running after you. What 'sitting' means here
is sitting yourself down for religious concerns. [Even]
if a man be running, if he is running for [purposes of]
religion then he is sitting. [And even] when sitting, if
he is sitting for [concerns of] this world he is running.
Supposing a man has ten matters of concern, let him
be concerned [only] with religion. God will [then]
attend to the other concerns without him needing
to attend to them. The Prophets were not concerned

with fame or with bread; their sole concern was
to seek the good pleasure of God, and they gained
both fame and bread [as well]. Anyone who seeks God's
good pleasure will be with the Prophets in this world
and the Hereafter. He will be the close companion of
*'those to whom God has been bountiful, the Prophets,
the totally sincere, and the martyrs'* (Qur'an 4: 69).
What place is there for [saying] that? He will be sitting
with God, Who has said: 'I am the Close Companion
of him who remembers Me' (*Ḥadīth Qudsī*). Were
God not sitting with him, there would have
been no desire for God in his heart.
(FMF no. 49, 184; DOR 192–193; SOTU 192–193)

*G*od addresses to humankind in general a reminder
that all things are in His keeping and there is nothing
we can obtain by ourselves (Qur'an 35: 15): '*O
humankind, you are the poor in relation to Allah and
He is the Infinitely Rich, the All-Praiseworthy.*' Such
is the relationship between the contingent and the
Absolute. The main message presented above evokes
the main theme of a classic Sufi treatise, *al-Tanwīr fī
isqāṭ al-tadbīr* ('The Illumination on the Elimination
of Self-Determination') by Shaykh Aḥmad Ibn ʿAṭāʾ
Allāh al-Iskandarī, best known as the author of *al-
Ḥikam al-ʿAṭāʾiyya*, maxims on key points of *sulūk* or
spiritual wayfaring. It also resembles a passage in one
of the letters (*Rasāʾil*) of the great twelfth century AH
(eighteenth century CE) Moroccan Shaykh Mawlāy
al-ʿArabī al-Darqāwī:

If you wish what you need to be given you without your having to search for it, turn away from it and concentrate on your Lord; you will receive it if God wills. And if you gave up your needs entirely and were occupied only with God, He would give you all the good things you wish for in this world and in the other; you would walk in Heaven as well as on the earth; and more than that, since the Prophet (on him be blessings and peace) has said, in the very words of his Lord, 'He who by remembering Me is distracted from his petition will receive more than those who ask.'*

As Mawlānā Jalāl al-Dīn himself puts it (*Mathnawī* III, 3210–3212):

Where there is pain, the cures will come;
Where there is poverty, riches will follow.

Where questions are, answers will be given;
Where ships are, there will be flowing water.

Don't spend so much time seeking water.
Be thirsty;
Then it will pour from above and below you.

---

* Translation by Burckhardt, T., *Letters of a Sufi Master* (Bedfont, UK: Perennial Books, 1969), p. 17.

3

Bring your Heart to My Door

God's Hands' connection with the Infinite Sea
Is perfect beyond any 'Like what?' or 'How?'

That connection's beyond being put into words.
To describe it is too great a task. That is all!

Rich man, you may bring a hundred sacks of gold;
But God will say, 'Loaded man, bring me your heart!

If your heart is pleased with you then I am pleased.
If it's against you, I'm against you as well.

It's not you that I look into: it is your heart.
O dear soul, bring that as your gift to My door.'
(M V, 879–883)

What do we have that we can possibly offer to our Creator, who promises such bounty, distributed from the infinite resources of the Universal Sea, to those who succeed in fulfilling the purpose of this worldly life? This life is not, after all, a game that will be won by 'the player who ends up with the most toys.' Indeed, the Holy Qur'an reminds us that this life is not a game at all in that sense. Admittedly, in one *āya* (Qur'an 29: 64) God says: '*This worldly life is but a pastime and a game, and truly the Abode of the Hereafter is life in truth, did they but know.*' The chief message to be taken from these words, however, is that from the viewpoint of Eternity it is only a fleeting moment and that worldly success is ultimately of no consequence: all that counts is whether we are acceptable to the Creator.

In the third *bayt* or couplet, Mawlānā Jalāl al-Dīn presents an important idea: if our hearts are pleased with us then God Himself will be pleased with us. In the end, our hearts will bear witness to whether we have fulfilled the *amāna* or trust of faith placed in us as human beings (see Qur'an 6: 130). Wealth and children will be of no avail if one does not come before the Creator '*with a sound heart*' (Qur'an 26: 89): one that is surrendered and at peace with Reality.

Though God does not *need* anything, what He *wants* from us is that our hearts be devoted to Him alone. Does He not have the right to expect that of His creation, when everything they have comes from His Hands, and from His 'Infinite Sea'? It has been said that if we truly understood the value of our hearts, we would think no sacrifice too great to make in order to purify them. It is in the mirror of a pure heart that the beauty and magnificence of the supra-sensory realms of Existence can be seen. For the One who already possesses every perfection a mirror is the only fitting gift, as we read in a story elsewhere in this book: 'What Can we Give the One Who Has Everything?'

4

Divine Generosity

Something that does not [even] enter the human
imagination is called a gift, for anything that passes
through the imagination is in proportion to one's level
of aspiration and worth. A Divine gift, however, is
in proportion to God's worth. Hence the gift is that
which is fitting for God, not that which can fit into the
imagination, or the aspiration, of God's servant. 'That
which no eye has seen and no ear has heard, nor has it
occurred to mortal minds ...'. In other words, 'No
matter how much the eyes have seen, the ears have
heard, or the mind has conceived of the gift you expect
from Me, My giving is above and beyond all that.'
(FMF no. 31, 131; DOR 141–142; SOTU 138)

'*T*hat which no eye has seen and no ear has heard, nor
has it occurred to mortal minds ...' is part of a *Ḥadīth
Qudsī* or Divine Tradition, which begins with the
words 'I have prepared for My servants ...' (Bukhārī,
Ṣaḥīḥ). In one of his letters, Mawlānā Rūmī reminds
his correspondent that our Almighty Creator is the

source of everything one could possibly desire – and that since He has in store blessings that go beyond that, the truly intelligent seek the Infinite Source of all Good rather than any particular benefit:

> May God Most High make the good news which you wrote about the prelude to the greatest of all good news, since all good news in this world is a flashing ray from that delightful Good News. But for the radiance, the splendour, of that Good News, no good news in this world would have any taste; it would all taste like earth and straw. The rays of His Beneficence imparted wheat to straw, stars to smoke, and mankind's beauty to dust' [see the Commentary on the passage 'Unitive Vision' below].

> They also brought the good news that the partial beings that are spirits will be united with their hopes and desires. That is why people of true intellect, not content with that, seek for the infinite Root, Source, and Mine of those desires and goals. Thus they may attain those Roots through these branches, and realize that Ultimate Reality through this contingent thing.

God Seeks out His Beloved Ones

هیچ عاشـق خـود نباشـد وصـلْ جـو
کـه نـه معشـوقش بـود جویایِ او.
لیـک عشـقِ عاشـقان تـن زِه کنـد؛
عشـقِ معشـوقان خـوش و فربـه کند.
چـون دراین دل، برق بهرِ دوست جَست
اندر آن دل، دوستی می دان که هسـت.
در دلِ تـو مـهرِ حـقّ چونشـد دو تـو
هسـت حـقّ را بی گمـانی مهرِ تـو.
هیـچ بانگِ کـف زدن نـآیـد بَــدَر
از یـکی دسـتِ تـو بی دستی دگـر.

In reality no lover can seek union
Without his loved one seeking him;

But lovers' love makes bodies bowstring-thin;
The love of loved ones makes them fresh and plump.
When love for the Beloved shoots like lightning
Into this heart, know that there's love in that heart.

When love for God has been doubled in your heart,
There can be no doubt that God has love for you.

No sound of clapping comes from one hand
Of yours without help from the other hand.

(M III, 4393–4397)

*T*he expression conventionally translated as 'union' does not mean that anyone or anything can be wholly united with God. What is meant is a seeker attaining the greatest possible nearness to Him through direct, experiential knowledge (*maʿrifa*) as distinct from merely rational, theoretical knowledge. This is the prize for the sake of which lovers seeking the Creator wear themselves out, becoming wan and gaunt in the way so often evoked in the poetry of worldly and mystical love.

Which came first: God's love for man, or man's love for God? Islam teaches that God is the Creator of all actions and all attributes, in whatever form they may be manifested. The most complete form manifested in creation is that of the human, who is a microcosm – a universe in miniature: '*And Allah created you and that which you do*' (Qur'an 37: 96). But for the Divine love and concern for humankind – '*and We have ennobled the children of Adam*' (Qur'an 17: 70) – humans would not be capable of love. Divine love for mankind is discussed in the preface to Book II of the *Mathnawī*, in which the author cites the Qur'anic phrase (5: 54) '*He loves them and they love Him*' as evidence that the Divine Love for His creatures necessarily precedes their love for Him:

Someone asked, 'What is being in love (ʿ*Āshiqī chīst*)?' I said, 'When you become like us, you will know.' Love is affection without reckoning, for which reason it has been said that it is in reality an Attribute of God, and only metaphorical, borrowed when applied to His servants. '*He loves them*' is the whole story (*tamāmast*), so what is left for (*kudāmast*) '*they love Him*'?

It is interesting to compare this with a passage in Discourse 42 (p. 257) of Shaykh ʿAbd al-Qādir al-Jīlānī's *Jalā' al-khawāṭir* ('The Removal of Cares'), as translated by Muhtar Holland (*raḥimah Allāh*):

At this point someone asked: 'Do you see love [*maḥabbah*] as being experienced in the first instance because of an involuntary compulsion [*iḍtirāran*] or by an act of free choice [*ikhtiyāran*]?' By way of reply, the Shaikh (may Allah be well pleased with him)

went on to say: 'In the case of a few isolated
individuals, the Lord of Truth (Almighty and
Glorious is He) simply casts His gaze upon
them and He loves them. He shifts them from
one thing to another in a single instant ... He
loves them in a single moment, so they love
Him too, of necessity. They notice that all
the blessings they have received come from
Him, not from any other. They notice all
His kindness and tender loving care, and all
the gifts He bestows on them, so they love
Him promptly and immediately, without any
gradual process or passage of time. For the
vast majority, however, it is a matter of choice.
Lovers begin to choose Allah (Exalted is He)
in preference to His creatures, then they start
choosing Him in preference not only to this
world, but also to the hereafter.'

The main difference between what Shaykh
ʿAbd al-Qādir says and what Mawlānā Jalāl al-Dīn
says, may God be pleased with them and with all
His *awliyā*', arises from the fact that the former is
speaking not from the perspective of ontology but
from that of *sulūk*, spiritual wayfaring. In some cases
Divine Attraction (*jadhb*) predominates, in others it
is striving (*mujāhada*) accompanied by progressive
'witnessing' (*mushāhada*).

All praiseworthy attributes belong essentially
to God and only metaphorically to humans; and

al-Wadūd (The Most Loving) is one of the Divine Names. Likewise, since loving is an act, and essentially there can only be one Actor, a creature's love for God must be 'borrowed from' God's love for Himself, which ontologically precedes His love for His creation.

6

What Can we Give the One Who Has Everything?

A friend of Joseph of Egypt returned from a journey.
'What have you brought me as a gift?' asked Joseph.
'What is there that you do not already have, and that you
are in need of?' his friend replied. 'Still, because there is
nothing more beautiful than you I have brought a mirror
so that you may behold your face in it at any time.' What
is there that God Most High does not have, and He is
in need of? One must bring to God a heart that shines,
so that He may see Himself in it. '*God does not look at
your forms or your actions; He looks at your hearts.*'
(FMF no. 50, 186; DOR 195; SOTU 195–196)

'J oseph of Egypt' means the Prophet Joseph, son of
the Prophet Jacob, son of the Prophet Isaac, son of
the Prophet Abraham, peace and blessings be upon
them all. As related in Surah 12 of the Qur'an and in

Prophetic Tradition, Joseph (in Arabic, Yūsuf) was a man of extraordinary beauty. In mediaeval times, a common type of mirror took the form of a disc of steel, polished to produce a reflective surface which from time to time would require re-polishing. The comparison of the (non-physical) human heart to a mirror appears to be evoked in a hadith (Bayhaqī, *Shuʿab al-īmān*) according to which the Prophet, peace and blessings be upon him, stated that 'There is a polish (*ṣayqal*) for everything, and the polish for the heart is the remembrance of God (*Dhikr Allāh*).'

'I was a Hidden Treasure and I desired to be known; so I created creation so that I might be known.' So runs a saying frequently quoted by Sufis. Though often cited as a Divine Tradition, it is more probably a veridical piece of inspired wisdom. Also relevant to the subject is this verse of the Qur'an (51: 56), quoted in a passage from the *Mathnawī* found elsewhere in this book: '*I created jinn and mankind only to serve Me.*' According to one well-known interpretation of the verse, 'to serve' here means 'to know' (some translators have written 'to worship', but despite what the author says in the same passage it is arguable that worship as such is not the entire purpose of our creation). While some knowledge is a matter of mental cognition and learning, much of the knowledge of God is in the nature of things at a higher level: that of the heart. It is there that we contemplate Him and He contemplates us. As the author concludes: 'One must bring to God a heart that shines, so that He may see Himself in it. "God does not look at your forms or your actions; He looks at your hearts."' (According to a hadith in Muslim's *Ṣaḥīḥ*, 'God does not look at your forms or your wealth; He looks at your hearts and your deeds.')

The Divine Transformer

O true lovers, O true lovers, I can transmute
dirt into jewels.
O you minstrels, O you minstrels, I fill your
tambourines with gold.

O thirsty ones, O thirsty ones, today I shall pour
out the drink;
I transform this dry rubbish-heap into Heaven
and Kawthar's Pool.

O friendless ones, O friendless ones, *relief has
come, relief has come*!
All who are heart-sore, sorrowful I turn into
sultans, Sanjars.

O elixir, O elixir, just look at Me, for I transform
A hundred cloisters into mosques, a hundred
gallows to pulpits.

O unbelievers, O unbelievers, I unlock your
locks for you.
I'm Absolute Sovereign; I create both believers
and infidels.

O Bū l-ʿAlāʾ, O Bū l-ʿAlāʾ, in Our hands
    you're a piece of wax.
Be a sword, I'll make a cup of you; be a cup,
    I'll make a sword of you.

From a sperm-drop you became a blood-clot,
    then grew so fair of form.
Come to Me, you human being, and I'll make
    you more lovely still.

I turn grief into rejoicing; I am the Guide
    for those who're lost.
I transform wolves into Josephs; I turn
    poison into sugar.

Master drinkers, master drinkers, I have
    opened the Secret's mouth
To unite every mouth that is dry with the
    lip of this Goblet.

O flower garden, O flower garden, gather
    flowers from My Garden;
There and then and I'll plant your fragrant
    herbs beside the water-lily.

O heaven, O heaven, you'll be more wide-
    eyed than a narcissus
When I transform dust into ambergris and
    thorns into jasmines.

O Universal Intellect, say what you will,
    you speak the truth.
You are the ruler, you are Ḥātim. Now
    I have no more to say.

                     (D III, 168–169)

*T*hese verses celebrate the power of Divine Omnipotence to transform things and situations in a trice, out of pure generosity. God responds to those in need, even if they are too burdened with cares to ask Him (although He loves to be asked). Those facing problems should never despair, for need itself calls forth a response – a theme explored elsewhere in this *Treasury*, in 'Do not Give Up Hope' and 'Why Trials Come our Way.'

The Pool of Kawthar is among the main features of Paradise. According to the Qur'an (108: 1), it is a Divine gift to the Prophet Muhammad, peace and blessings be upon him. Anyone who drinks from it will never thirst again (Muslim, *Ṣaḥīḥ*; Bukhārī, *Ṣaḥīḥ*). Mawlānā Rūmī uses the name Bū l-ʿAlā, or Abū l-ʿAlā', not to denote any specific individual but to mean 'So-and-So'. A sword embodies combative activity, whereas a cup embodies passive receptivity. The name Ḥātim belongs to the paradigm of chivalry and generosity among the Arabs: the pre-Islamic Bedouin Ḥātim al-Ṭā'ī, renowned for the immense sacrifices he made in providing for his guests according to the highest traditions of Arab hospitality. The 'master drinkers' are those dedicated to the search for direct knowledge of God, something not attainable by human effort but only through pure Divine Generosity: *'they do not embrace anything of His Knowledge save by His permission'* (Qur'an 2: 255). Fragrant herbs symbolize the intimation of mystical knowledge, and are mentioned in the Qur'an as being among the delights of Paradise. The lotus or water-lily is a universal symbol of perfect purity and of enlightenment.

The Universal Intellect is the highest of those levels of God's infinite Knowledge that are potentially accessible to human beings. Since it is a pure reflection of Truth its authority is beyond question; since knowledge of the Divine is the finest of gifts, its generosity is boundless.

ASPECTS OF UNITY: WISDOM, KNOWLEDGE, SERENITY

Existence is One

We are like flutes, and the music in us is
from You;
We are like mountains, and the echo in us
is from You.

We are like chess-pieces caught up in victory
or defeat:
Both come from You, Whose Attributes shine
with beauty!

Who are we, O You who are the soul of our souls,
That we should continue to exist beside You?

We and our existences are really non-existences:
You are the Absolute Being who manifests
the transient.

We are all lions, but lions on a banner:
because of the wind
They go rushing onward from moment
to moment.

Their onrush is visible, the wind is unseen:
May the unseen thing not become absent from us!

Both the wind that moves us and our being
are granted by You:
Our whole existence comes from You
bringing us into being.

(M I, 599–605)

*H*ere Jalāl al-Dīn Rūmī, while addressing the Almighty, states and illustrates a doctrine. If everything in the universe is contingent upon His Attributes and actions – for nothing else can exist of its own accord – then the act of existing can ultimately be attributed only to its source, which is the Divine Action. The acts of created things, in this perspective, are 'acquired' and contingent. That must then apply to the act of existing (*wujūd*), as it does to any other act. *'And God created you and that which you do'* (Qur'an 37: 96).

What You Do is What You Get

Whatever happens to you, train yourself, in case you
need to do battle with somebody every day. Others may
say that 'All is from God', but we say that necessarily
chastizing one's ego and abstaining from the world are
also from God. This is like [the story of] a man who
shook apricots down from a tree and ate them. When
the owner of the orchard found out he said, 'Don't
you fear God?' 'Why should I?' answered the man.
'The tree belongs to God, and I, a servant of God, am
eating of what is His.' 'Then I must respond to you,'
said the owner. 'Bring me some rope, tie him to this
tree, and beat him until [my] response is clear [to him].'
'Don't *you* fear God?' cried the man. 'Why should I?'
asked the owner of the orchard. 'You are God's
servant, and this is God's stick I am beating
His servant with.'

What this shows is that the world is like a mountain.
Everything you say, be it good or evil, is echoed by
that mountain. If you imagine that you made a
pleasant sound but the mountain gave an ugly

reply, it is absurd to think that a nightingale could sing to the mountain and that it could reply with the voice of a crow, a human, or a donkey. Know for certain, therefore, that it was from you that the donkey noise came.

> When you come to the mountain, make a
> pleasant sound.
> Why bray at the mountain like a donkey?
> (FMF no. 40, 151–152; DOR 160; SOTU 158)

*T*his is an interesting example of the way in which Rūmī in his discourses sometimes makes a subtle transition from one theme to another. In this passage there are two such shifts. There is, of course, a connection between the need for constant self-training and the uncomfortable truths of individual human responsibility, on the one hand, and of necessary consequences on the other: 'as you sow, so shall you reap.' As was seen in the story of the thief and the magistrate (see 'God's Decree'), it is not an acceptable excuse for wrongdoing to say that it was decreed by God. It is no defence for the man who steals from the apricot tree to say that the tree belongs to God, since the Sacred Law gives people the right to own and control property, and prescribes penalties for those who take it without permission. Resuming the original theme, Mawlānā underlines that whatever reaction we receive from the world is just an 'echo', the world's response to our words and deeds.

3

Remembrance of God (Dhikr Allāh) Brings Everlasting Benefits

The senses' light and our immortal souls
Do not perish or vanish completely, like grass.

But just like the stars or the light of the moon,
All of them are erased by the sun's brilliant rays.

God's remembrance is water, and time is a wasp:
Remembering 'So-and-So', female or male.

Hold your breath in the water of *dhikr* and persist,
To escape those worn-out thoughts and obsessions.

And so those who have passed away from this world
Have not perished but been absorbed in [God's] Traits.

Their attributes have all vanished without trace
In God's Attributes, like stars before the sun.
(M IV 422–423, 437–438, 442–443)

*A*s explained in 'Three Categories of Creatures', the human soul contains aspects of angelic as well as animal nature, and human consciousness has been created for everlasting life Hereafter. After death, 'the lamp of the human spirit' lives on. In speaking of 'the senses' light' not perishing, Rūmī means that the light that enabled a person's senses to operate in their lifetime continues to exist after death. But just as the light of the sun overcomes that of the moon and stars, the irruption of truth that follows our departure from this world of illusions eclipses, so to speak, those sense-impressions which previously dominated our consciousness. Conversely, the realm of meanings that tends to seem abstract, even remote, to most people in this world becomes overwhelmingly real in the Afterlife. The Truth dawns on us, and now we see the Light.

But what has all this to do with *Dhikr Allāh*, the Remembrance of God? Mawlānā shows us, using a striking image. Imagine all the desires and concerns of this world, the 'worn-out thoughts and obsessions', as wasps that are chasing you. Seeking to escape them, you pay heed to the warning '*So flee unto God*' (Qur'an 51: 50): you run towards the Eternal, taking refuge in the Remembrance that brings tranquillity to the heart (13: 28); it is like a stream in which you hide under the surface, breathing through a straw until the wasps have given up and dispersed. In his ghazals, Mawlānā describes more aspects of the blessings and benefits of *Dhikr Allāh*. Here is one example, concerning invocation of the Divine Name (*Dīwān*, vol. 6, p. 165; from ghazal 2892):

> 'His Name is life to all souls, His *Dhikr* the ruby in mines.
> Love for Him in the soul provides security and hope.
>
> When I invoke His Name, fresh good fortune comes my way:
> The Name's become the Named, without duality or delay.'

Lastly, Rūmī points out that for those who devoted themselves wholeheartedly to *Dhikr Allāh* in their earthly lifetime, the benefits may become unimaginably greater in the Hereafter. If all their human attributes have been effaced by the Divine Attributes, to the greatest extent possible, their individuality has become absorbed in the imperishable Light of God, like the stars in sunlight.

4

Unitive Vision

How could you know what kind of King is
inwardly my bosom friend?
Pay no heed to my golden-yellow face; my
legs are made of iron!

I've turned my face entirely to the Sovereign
One who produced me.
For Him who has created me (*āfarīdastam*) I have
a thousand forms of praise (*āfarīn*).

Sometimes I am bright as the sun; sometimes
I'm like a sea of pearls.
Within I have the skies' glory; outside, the
earth's humility.

Inside the jar of this world I am wandering
around like a bee.
Don't notice just my buzzing drone: I have a
house that's honey-filled!

If you're in search of us, dear heart, ascend to
the sky's blue-green dome;
My fortress is such a palace that I'm *the
safest of the safe.*

How fearsome is the water that causes the
heavens' mill to turn!
Being the mill-wheel in that water, I cry
sweetly as I turn.

Since you see demons and mankind and jinn
are all at my command,
Do you not know that I am Solomon, with his
seal on my ring?

How could I become withered, when every
part of me has blossomed?
Why should I be a donkey's slave? Burāq's
saddled for me to ride!

Why should I be less than the moon, when no
scorpion has struck my foot?
Why should I not climb out of this well, when
I have a firm rope to hold?

For pigeon spirits I have built a pigeon house.
O spirit-bird,
Fly this way, for I have a hundred impregnable
towers.

Though I wander from house to house, yet
I am the sun's flashing rays;
Though born of water and clay, I am agates,
rubies, and gold.

Whatever pearl you catch sight of, look for
another pearl inside.
For every speck of dust says, 'There is a
treasure buried in me.'

Each pearl will say to you, 'Do not content
yourself with my beauty;
The light I have upon my brow comes from
the candle of the mind.'

Now I will be silent, for you have not the
wits to understand.
Don't nod to try and trick me, for my eyes
can tell if wits are there!

(D III, 1426)

For some of His servants, His 'bosom friends', God opens up a station of beholding (*mashhad*) beyond the normal senses. Whatever they encounter in creation they see in its relation to the totality, the oneness of Being, and they hear it speaking with the voice of its inner state. The exclamation 'How fearsome is the water that causes the heavens' mill to turn!' evokes such a state of vision; 'Being the mill-wheel in that water' evokes a sense of oneness. That water is fearsome because it is vast, momentous, unceasing; it is the manifestation of the Divine Decree.

A yellow face implies sorrow and weakness. Legs of iron stand for strength and endurance. God gave The Prophet-King Solomon, peace be upon him, dominion over mankind, jinn and the animal kingdom. The poet, by virtue of his eminent state, has become a spiritual king, with creation at his beck and call. As a spiritual guide he summons souls, which are like homing-pigeons, to his place of refuge. Burāq is the heavenly steed on which the Prophet (*ṣallā Allāh ʿalayh wa sallam*) was borne on his Night Journey (*Isrāʾ*) and Ascension (*Miʿrāj*). The 'well' that the poet can climb out of is this lower world. Though 'born of water and clay' he has been transformed into gems; it was believed that the rays of the sun and stars acted on lower substances beneath the Earth's surface, transforming them into jewels and precious metals. The sun's rays move from one roof to the next as it traverses the sky during the daylight hours.

'*Naught is there but glorifies His praise, but you understand not their glorification*' (Qurʾan 17: 44) applies to all but those who are granted this station of beholding; hence the exclamation in the last couplet.

5

The Silence of the Ocean

Silence is like an ocean, and speech like a river.
The Ocean is seeking you; don't seek the river.

For all who've attained to looking at God,
All this information is no longer needed.

And once you are sitting with your Beloved
Then you may send the matchmakers away.
(M IV 2062, 2067–2068)

*T*his passage from the *Mathnawī*, like so many in
the author's *Dīwān*, evokes a spiritual state. At the
same time it conveys a didactic message. Speech is
like a river in the sense that it is passing, sequential,
limited. Silence is like an ocean in the sense that it
is not limited in the same way; poetically speaking,
the ocean represents infinity. There are moments in

life when the only thing to do is to still the mind and tongue and to concentrate on the Divine Presence.

The second half-line reminds us of a truth noted elsewhere in this selection. If we come to be engaged in seeking for the Perfect, the Infinite One, that is only possible because He is already seeking us. The river is finite and transient; it is forever running, and the water that we see in it now is not the same water we saw in it seconds ago. The Ocean, though, is vast; and the Ocean of God's bounty and compassion is infinite.

If we ever attain direct, unmediated knowledge of the Lord of the Universe we shall no longer need information or direction from others. We shall be able, God willing, to see for ourselves. Blessed with the ability to realize experientially His Presence with us and ours with Him, we may 'sit with' the Beloved without any need for a go-between.

6

The Ultimate Goal

All things are causally linked (*musalsal*) to God,
Glorious and Majestic. It is He who is sought on His
own account and desired for His own sake, not for
anything else. Since [God] is beyond all, better than all,
nobler than all, and subtler than all, how could He be
desired for the sake of something lesser than Him? So
'unto Him is the final End' (cf. Qur'an 53: 42). Once
they have reached Him they have attained their complete
objective, beyond which one cannot pass. This human
soul is a place of doubts and difficulties. Those doubts
and difficulties cannot be removed from it by any means
unless it falls in love. Then no doubts or difficulties
remain in it, for *'Your love for a thing makes
you blind and deaf [to all others].'*
(FMF no. 23, 101; DOR 112–113; SOTU 105–106)

*T*his passage includes two of the primary themes
of Mawlānā Jalāl al-Dīn's message: what it is we
exist for, and what we should do about it. God is
the Origin, the meaning, the Purpose of Existence.
No one and nothing can take the place of Him. To

fail to realize this is to miss the point of one's own existence. Our purpose as humans is to serve Him and to know Him. Everything that one can possibly admire, love and desire is to be found in Him, Exalted and Transcendent is He. God created Love to be a means for His creatures to be attracted to one another, give them comfort in their worldly lives, and ensure the perpetuation of their kind. Beyond that, He created Love, a force that can overcome 'doubts and difficulties', the myriad complexities of the human soul, and propel us towards Himself. He alone is the fitting object of our ultimate aspirations, and *'unto Him is the final End'*.

7

Silent Joy

اَبْشِرُواْ يَا قَوْمُ هَذَا فَتْحُ بَابِ

قَدْ نَجَوْتُمْ مِنْ شَتَاتِ الِاغْتِرَابِ

اِفْرَحُواْ قَدْ جَاءَ «مِيقَاتُ الرِّضَا»

مِنْ حَبِيبٍ «عِنْدَهُ أُمُّ الْكِتَابِ»

قَالَ «لَا تَاسَوْاْ عَلَى مَا فَاتَكُمْ»

اِذْ بَدَى بَدْرٌ خَرُوقٌ لِلْحِجَابِ

ذَا مُنَاخٌ أُوقِفُواْ بِعُرَانِنَا

ذَا نَعِيمٌ لَيْسَ يُحْصِيهِ الْحِسَابُ

اِنَّ فِي عُتْبِ الْهَوَا اَلْفُ الْوَفَا

اِنَّ فِي صَمْتِ الْوَلَا لُطْفُ الْخِطَابِ

قَدْ سَكَتْنَا فَافْهَمُواْ سِرَّ السُّكُوتِ

يَا كِرَامُ اللهُ اَعْلَمُ بِالصَّوَابِ

O Folk, rejoice, for the Door is now open.
You're safe from any kind of alienation.

Be joyful; the time is here for our acceptance
By the Beloved *'with Whom is the Mother-Book'*.

He said *'Sorrow not over what has escaped you'*:
The full moon rose, piercing the veils with its light.

Here camels rest. Settle in our camping-grounds.
This is bliss that is too immense to be reckoned.

Bearing blame for your love proves loyalty;
In a devotee, silence is subtle speech.

Now we're silent. Understand silence's secret,
O noble friends. 'God knows best what is true.'
(D I, 193; no. 320)

he Folk' (*al-Qawm*) is an expression used to refer
to the Sufis collectively. The Beloved *'with Whom is
the Mother-Book'* is God Himself, *who 'deletes what
He will and confirms what He will'* (Qur'an 13: 39):
His infinite Knowledge comprehends all matters in
the minutest detail, and yet out of His Mercy and
Generosity He grants acceptance to whomever He
wills and forgives their shortcomings. *'Sorrow not
over what escaped you'* comes from the first clause
of Qur'an 57: 23, *'That you sorrow not over what
escaped you.'* Those blessed with the assurance of

eternal happiness no longer have cause to regret past misfortunes or missed opportunities.

This poem reads like an evocation of entering Paradise. It captures the sense of a moment of serene triumph in the certainty of forgiveness, security and completeness. The call for silence in the final couplet is characteristic; many of Rūmī's poems end in a similar tone. When all is said and done, whatever kind of commentary one may attempt on the writings of one of the supreme spiritual authors of all time is no substitute for readers' own reflections. And 'God knows best what is true.'

Further Reading

The now immense volume of publications relating (to a greater or lesser degree) to Mawlānā Rūmī includes a good number of worthwhile works in English; this list presents only a small selection, along with Persian text editions for readers of that language.

Persian Texts

Istiʿlāmī, Muḥammad (ed. and comm.), *Mathnawī*, 7 vols. (Tehran: Sukhan, 1379/2000).

Nicholson, R. A. (ed., tr., and comm.), *The Mathnawí of Jalálu'ddín Rúmí*, 6 vols. (London: Luzac, 1925–40). The pioneering critical edition. The translation (though rather slavish) and commentary also remain valuable. All references in this *Treasury* are to Nicholson's edition.

Subḥānī, Tawfīq (ed.), *Majālis-i sabʿa (Haft khiṭāba)* (Tehran: Kayhān, 1351/1972).

——— (ed.), *Maktūbāt* (Tehran: Markaz-i Nashr-i Dānishgāhī, 1371/1992).

Furūzānfar, Badīʿ al-Zamān (ed.), *Kulliyyāt-i Shams yā Dīwān-i kabīr*, 10 vols. (Tehran: Dānishgāh-i Tihrān, 1336–46/1957–67).

——— (ed.), *Kitāb-i Fīh mā fīh* (Tehran: Amīr-i Kabīr, 1348/1969).

Muwaḥḥid, Muḥammad ʿAlī (ed.), *Maqālāt-i Shams-i Tabrīzī* (Tehran: Khwārazmī, 1369/1990).

Humāʾī. Jalāl al-Dīn (ed.), *Walad-nāma, az Sultān Walad* (Tehran: Humā, 1376/1997).

Studies

Chittick, W. C., *The Sufi Path of Love: The Spiritual Teachings of Rumi* (Albany: State University of New York Press (SUNY), 1983).

Gamard, I., *Rumi and Islam: Selections from His Stories, Poems and Discourses* (Woodstock, VT: SkyLight Paths Publishing, 2004).

Keshavarz, F., *Reading Mystical Lyric: The Case of Jalal al-Din Rumi* (Columbia, SC: University of South Carolina Press, 1998).

Lewis, F. D., *Rumi Past and Present, East and West: The Life, Teachings and Poetry of Jalāl al-Din Rumi*, revised ed. (Oxford: Oneworld, 2008).

Safavi, S. G. and S. Weightman, *Rūmī's Mystical Design: Reading the Mathnawī, Book One* (Albany, NY: SUNY, 2009).

Schimmel, A., *The Triumphal Sun: A Study of the Works of Jalāloddin Rumi*, revised ed. (Albany, NY: SUNY, 1993).

Waley, M. I., 'Mawlana Jalal al-Din Rumi and Islamic Spirituality', *Livejournal* [website], 25 November 2006. «https://hojja-nusreddin.livejournal.com/1121514.html», accessed 24 May 2019. Originally published in *Islamica* issue 13, in 2006.

Translations

Arberry, A. J. (tr.), *Discourses of Rumi*, reprint (Richmond, UK: Curzon Press, 1995). The original English version, stylistically pleasing and showing a wide knowledge of Islam. Avoid the adaptation, available online, which contains serious distortions.

Chittick, W. C. (tr.), *Me and Rumi: the Autobiography of Shams-i Tabrizi* (Louisville, KY: Fons Vitae, 2004).

Gamard, I. and R. Farhadi (ed. and tr.), *The Quatrains of Rumi* (San Rafael, CA: Sufi Dari Books, 2008).

Mojaddedi, J. (tr.), *The Masnavi, Book One*, with an introduction and notes (Oxford; New York: Oxford World Classics, 2004). Also, from the same translator and publisher, *The Masnavi, Book Two* (2007), *The Masnavi, Book Three* (2014), *The Masnavi, Book Four* (2018). Verse translations, which some will prefer although they often depart from the literal meaning. Mojaddedi takes liberties and lacks gravitas but is lively, learned, and ingenious.

Rifai, K., *Listen: Commentary on the Spiritual Couplets of Mevlana Rumi*, tr. V. Holbrook (Louisville, KY: Fons Vitae, 2011). Masterly commentary, in the Ottoman tradition, on Book I, couplets 1–4048.

Thackston, W. M. (tr.), *Signs of the Unseen: Discourses of Jalaluddin Rumi* (Putney, VT; Boston, MA: Shambhala, 1994). Less elegant than Arberry, but good and based on a superior edition of the Persian text.

Waley, M. I. (tr.), *'Seven Sermons'* (Majālis-i sab'a). Forthcoming.

Williams, A. (tr.), *Spiritual Verses* (London, New York: Penguin Classics, 2007). A sound, very readable prose translation of Book I by a long-time Rūmī specialist.

Selections

Arberry, A. J. (tr.), *Tales from the Masnavi* (London: Allen & Unwin, 1961).

—— (tr.), *More Tales from the Masnavi* (London: Allen & Unwin, 1963).

Dunn, P., M. Dunn Mascetti, and R. A. Nicholson (tr.), *The Illustrated Rumi: A Treasury of Wisdom from the Poet of the Soul* (New York: HarperCollins, 2000).

Mabey, J. (ed.), *Rumi: A Spiritual Treasury* (London: Oneworld, 2000).

Nicholson, R. A. (tr.), *Rūmī, poet and mystic, 1207–1273. Selections from his Writings* (London: Allen and Unwin, 1950).

Index